Advance Praise for
To My Beloveds

"In this intimate and life-churning call to hope, to healing and to ourselves, Reverend Jen Bailey offers all of what makes her a leader and believer built for these times... whispering to us in every word the ancestral wisdom that we, her readers, are built for them too."

—Dawn-Lyen Gardner, actor and activist

"Rev. Jennifer Bailey is preternaturally wise and tenderly prophetic—a visionary tending redemptive possibilities within our present of disarray. *To My Beloveds* is a wildly beautiful and nourishing introduction of her voice to a wider world. It is a stunning offering of public theology from and for a new generation, yet it could not be more vigorously, lovingly rooted in deep time and place and lineage. This book is a cause for rejoicing."

—Krista Tippett, Founder & CEO of the On Being Project, host of *On Being*, and curator of The Civil Conversations Project

"I could not put this book down. The stories are piercing, the counsel felt both urgent and eternal, the writing shimmers. Jen Bailey is a generational voice."

—Eboo Patel, Founder and President, IFYC and author of *Acts of Faith*

"Jen Bailey's radical hope points us to joy that can be found in both the mourning and the morning if we take the necessary steps of living into the gifts God has planted in each of us. This book is a moving witness to the power of holy change and transformation."

—Emilie M. Townes, Dean and Distinguished Professor of Womanist Ethics and Society, Vanderbilt Divinity School

"Jen Bailey is wise, and a gifted writer too. For both the spiritual misfit and tradition-lover, Jen's story and prophetic vision will open your heart, sharpen your mind, and prepare your spirit. We are lucky to be her Beloveds."

—Casper ter Kuile, author, *The Power of Ritual,* and co-host of the podcast

"I am continually impressed and mesmerized by the genius of Jennifer Bailey. I have learned so much from her since I met her in divinity school, and this book catapulted me into another realm of healing and self-reflection. I cannot wait for everyone to get their hands on her book!"

—Prisca Dorcas Mojica Rodríguez, author of *For Brown Girls with Sharp Edges and Tender Hearts: A Love Letter to Women of Color*

"Black people need soft landing spaces of care, encouragement, and love. In *To My Beloveds: Letters on Faith, Race, Loss, and Radical Hope*, Jen Bailey invites us into the soft spaces in her life. Through intimate letters introducing us to her community, Jen carefully weaves emotions and words into beautiful love letters. *To My Beloveds* makes you smile with its familiar tone, hold your breath as you feel the heartache, and gives its readers hope beyond hope."

—Rev. Dr. Theresa S. Thames, Associate Dean of Religious Life and the Chapel, Princeton University

"In this stirring and beautifully written collection of letters, Jen invites us to go deeper into our own histories, deeper into our tightest held hopes, and deeper into transformative possibilities for the future. Her vulnerability and the wisdom she gleans from her ancestors and community will serve as a roadmap for creating a more equitable, just, and joyful world."

—Lindsey Krinks, author of *Praying with Our Feet: Pursuing Justice and Healing on the Streets*

"Intimate, powerful, and deeply wise, *To All My Beloveds* is a healing balm for the heart. I read them all in one night and will savor them for years to come. Let these sacred letters soothe you, awaken you, and inspire you!

—Valarie Kaur, author of *SEE NO STRANGER: A Memoir and Manifesto of Revolutionary Love*

"Bailey shows unflinching love in the midst of a wounded world. These are the kinds of letters that save lives."

—Rev. Tyler Ho-Yin Sit, Pastor and Author of *Staying Awake: The Gospel for Changemakers*

TO MY BELOVEDS

Letters on Faith, Race, Loss, and Radical Hope

By Jennifer Bailey

chalice
press

Saint Louis, Missouri

ChalicePress.com

Print: 9780827237278
EPUB: 9780827237285
EPDF: 9780827237292

chalice
press

Chalice Press, St. Louis,
Missouri, USA

For Mama and Max

Contents

Salutation

Dear Beloved-to-Be,

I was seven or eight years old when Sister Catherine Weldon pulled me aside one Sunday after church and said, "Baby, you gonna preach someday."

I do not remember the context for her declaration, but I'm sure it was partly inspired by our pastor, Reverend Pendelton, who was a youth ministry genius. Where some saw Black children as a problem that needed to be solved, he saw us as leaders with unique insights into the nature of God. He empowered us to use our voices and trained us early on the nuisances of leading worship services.

Maybe I'd prayed that day or read scripture. Perhaps I'd led the congregation in our weekly recitation of the Ten Commandments or the Apostles' Creed. It could have been the womanish way I directed the younger kids in the choir to stand up straight in their green and white robes as we sang the A&B selections that morning. Whatever it was that I'd done caused Sister Weldon's spiritual third eye to open and give witness to something in me that I did not see in myself.

That is one of the great gifts of community—the recognition that we do not emerge from our mother's womb fully formed, but rather are shaped by the ordinary encounters we have with the people whom we call *beloved*.

The term *beloved* appears 130 times in the *New Revised Standard Version* of the sacred text of my faith tradition—the Holy Bible. It is used as a salutation (the Pauline epistles), a demarcation of divine favor (Matthew 12:18), and a pet name between lovers (Song of Songs). In my life interactions, I use it in reference to those I have been called into sacred relationships: family, friends, lovers, ancestors, and those yet to be born. Some of them I have known intimately, while others exist only on the periphery of my dreams.

All are my teachers. Teachers like Sister Weldon.

I wish I could say that her words stuck with me that day. I'm sure I just smiled and nodded politely before chasing my friends Caronda and Vanessa down the back staircase of the sanctuary to play in the churchyard. My mama, who overheard the conversation, reminded me of Sister Weldon's prophecy in the days leading up to my ordination in the African Methodist Episcopal (AME) Church. As she helped me slip into my black preaching robe for the first time, she smiled and shared a message from Sister Weldon: "I told you so."

Seven years later, on February 2, 2021, Sister Weldon became an ancestor at the age of 92. Her obituary describes her as one who loved the earth, someone whose love of the land was evident in the time she spent fishing with her husband, taking her grandchildren camping, or working in her flower and vegetable gardens. Toward the end is a snapshot of the woman I knew—a lifelong member of the AME Church, a high soprano in the choir, a faithful member of the Women's Missionary Society, and an expert baker who loved bringing freshly made desserts on Sunday mornings. To that list I would add *seer*, *discerner of spirits,* and *wisdom keeper.*

Losing her during a global pandemic meant that I was not able to honor her life and legacy in person. Yet when I allow my memory to guide me on a journey into the past, tears of mourning give way to sweet release. I am a part of a spiritual tradition wherein death is not the counterpoint to life. It is an unfolding process that contextualizes, catalyzes, and confirms our relationship to time.

Time is the one resource we all share, though each of us never knows at a given moment how much of it we have left. Lately, I have been fantasizing about what it would be like to live a long life. That is why when people ask me what I want to be when I grow up, I say an old Black woman. I want to be the church mother, like Sister Weldon, wearing a big hat and seated at her designated pew every Sunday. I strive to be the lady who always has a ready supply of hard candies at the bottom of her purse and is equally equipped with a word of encouragement or correction for the young people who run past her in the sanctuary.

I want to be like the Black women at Bethel African Methodist Episcopal Church who helped raise me. They were Proverbs 18:21[1] women who knew that, for Black children, the power of life and death reside in the tongue. Each week they spoke life into me over Sunday school lessons and youth group expeditions. They whispered words of affirmation as my friends and I snuck into the church kitchen for an extra sweet roll or slice of pound cake after services.

Their lives were testimonies of survival in a world that refused to see the fullness of their humanity. These church women knew their God to be *real* even when their understanding of the Divine did not fit neatly within church doctrine. Exquisitely imperfect vessels, they were healers and heretics, master theologians and misfits who conjured the Spirit often and by many names—*Waymaker, Deliverer, Shelter in a Time of Storm,* and *A Present Help*

---

[1] Proverbs 18:21 reads "Death and life are in the power of the tongue, and those who love it will eat its fruits." (New Revised Standard Version).

in a Time of Trouble. Their God was one who, in the words of a gospel song from my youth, was "always on time," meaning no matter what we may see with our human eyes, the Spirit of the living God is always present and toiling on behalf of those in the margins.

They were not perfect. At times their own unaddressed trauma and complicity to the status quo led to opinions that were both loud *and* wrong. I did not, for example, learn about the hyper-sexualization of Black women's bodies from rap music videos as many throughout my childhood falsely asserted. I learned about it at the church. I remember as a young girl attending youth ministry conventions where older men with wandering hands insisted upon unsolicited hugs that lingered a little too long and comments offered a little too often regarding my blossoming figure. After one particularly unnerving episode with an older man at a church convention, I shared what happened with a church mother that I trusted. She proceeded to check the length of my hem, comment on the tightness of my blouse, and insist upon my wearing a lap cloth (a long piece of fabric made of satin and lace worn over a skirt) for the remainder of the service—lest I unwittingly lead one of the men into a state of temptation.

Even their imperfections were a gift that warned against the danger of placing a person on too high a pedestal. People, they taught me, will disappoint you. Even God sometimes may disappoint you. I learned that it's one thing to honor the achievements of a person, it's quite another to take stock of their values by carefully observing how they live. A famous preacher, they admonished, may speak a compelling word that leads a listener to Christ, but a community committed to walking with that believer through the best and worst of times will keep that person in the faith.

Indeed, the church women of my childhood did not wait for a savior or celebrity to come and fix their troubles. Their callused hands were both witness and warning. The hardened flesh of their palms told stories of labor seen and unseen. Their fingers worked miracles, turning simple ingredients into feasts that fed multitudes and fashioned hair some labeled "unruly" into intricate braided patterns that made us feel like African queens and kings. Guided by mother wit and determination, they created new family structures and reared children who were not theirs by blood.

These are the women who taught me grit. They also showed me that ingenuity, creativity, and play are always within our grasp. A blank piece of paper and set of crayons can be the gateway to a new world. A cardboard box can be transformed into a car, a house, and a spaceship, sometimes within the span of minutes. "Outside" can be a pulpit, a racetrack, a zoo, a safari, and a laboratory. And God, they shared, is present in all of it.

Annice Mallory

Catherine Sanders

Connie Fonza

Ella Oliver

Evelyn Manley

Gertrude Mallory

Jacqueline Watson

Johnetta Green

Karlean Lamotte

Loretta Jackson

Louise Watson

Marla Ferguson

Onelle Crider

Royce Warren

Shirley Palmer

Sonya Mallory

Venita Bowie

I speak your names.

Radical Hope as Roadmap

The church women of my childhood were progenitors of a lineage of social healing grounded in *radical hope*. For them, hope was and is not the same thing as optimism. It is not a feeling nor a desired future state that is the substance of our longings. Hope is the everyday practice of believing that the material conditions of the world can be better and that we have the capacity to bring about that change in the here and now.

This vision of hope is best captured in the words of organizer, educator, and curator Mariame Kaba. A longtime prison abolitionist, her work focuses on ending violence, dismantling the prison industrial complex, transformative justice, and supporting youth leadership development. In her book, *We Do This 'Til We Free Us: Abolitionist Organizing and Transforming Justice,* she recounts the story of how she learned the idea of *hope as a discipline*:

> The idea of hope being a discipline is something I heard from a nun many years ago who was talking about it in conjunction with making sure we were of the world and in the world. Living in the afterlife already in the present was kind of a form of escape; but that actually, it was really, really important for us to live in the world and be of the world. The hope that she was talking about was this grounded hope that was practiced every day; that people actually practiced it all the time.
>
> And so, I bowed to that. I heard that many years ago and then I felt the sense of, "Oh my god." That speaks to me as a philosophy of living, that hope is a discipline that we have to practice every single day. Because in our world, it's easy

to feel a sense of hopelessness, that everything is all bad all the time; that nothing is going to ever change; that people are evil and bad at the core. It feels sometimes that it's being proven in various, different ways, so I get that, so I really get that. I understand why people feel that way. I just choose differently. I choose to think a different way and I choose to act in a different way. I choose to trust people until they prove themselves untrustworthy.[2]

How is this definition of hope *radical*? Today we use the term "radical" most often in political contexts to describe a fundamental shift in policy (i.e., radical reform) or people on the extreme ends of an ideological spectrum (i.e., religious radicals). Yet, the origin of the word in the English language is the Latin *radicalis,* meaning "of or having roots." One of the earliest applications of the word was from the fourteenth century in the field of botany to refer to the literal roots of plants.

The hope of my foremothers is indeed rooted. Its tendrils reach deep into a history riddled with stories of trauma and triumph, grief and glee, drama and delight—from the coast of western Africa to the fields of the Mississippi Delta. I have a mentor who says that Black women in the United States have never had a vision of liberation that was not inclusive of everyone. This, despite the generations of violence, neglect, and abuse Black women have been subjected to in the United States.

Radical hope is just one expression of what Yolanda Pierce calls *grandmother theology*. Grandmother theology, according to Pierce, is a subset of womanist thought grounded in a generational wisdom that is only possible with a maturity forged by the

---

[2] Mariame Kaba, *We Do This 'Til We Free Us: Abolitionist Organizing and Transforming Justice* (Chicago: Haymarket Books, 2021), 26-27.

passage of time. It provides an alternative way to understand and know God by transporting us back two or more generations into informal sacred spaces where Black women's theological discourse was developed.[3] Places like the church kitchen, where Sister Weldon ministered to my friends and me.

Along the way, the church women in my life helped me uncover three characteristics of radical hope, each of which is tied to a central question that helps us assess the conditions before us.[4]

1. ***Memory as an antidote to death.*** Death is a necessary part of the life cycle. We live and thus we must die. The church mothers in my life taught me that in our tradition death was never final. The ability to access those who had transitioned from this life to the ancestral plane was as simple as calling their name. When we remember them, we transcend the limitations of time and space and allow their stories and experience to anchor and accompany us. Institutions, as entities formed by and made of people, are also subject to a life cycle. This means that they too inevitably must die in their current form. Collective memory helps us glean the lessons of our historical institutions, discern that which we can and should carry forward, and let go of that which no longer serves us.

   Question: *What is dying here?*

---

[3] Yolanda Pierce, *In My Grandmother's House*: *Black Women, Faith, and the Stories We Inherit* (Minneapolis: Broadleaf Books, 2021), xvii.

[4] These questions were inspired by a conversation with my friend and colleague M. Rako Fabionar during the *How We Deepen Retreat* at the Fetzer Institute (Kalamazoo, Michigan) in October 2019. In his work, Rako's work integrates developmental psychology, wisdom traditions, and cultural arts. He designs and facilitates trainings, experiences, and conferences for purpose-driven organizations and networks committed to equitable and regenerative futures. I am grateful to count him among the teachers I have had the privilege to learn from on this journey.

2. ***Imagination as a pathway to resurrection***. There are some
    institutions, ideologies, and theologies that are dead and
    need to stay that way. But for that we collectively deem
    worthy of preservation for the sake of our communal whole-
    ness and wellbeing, there is a way to breathe new life into
    it. We simply need to open the eyes of our imagination to
    see beyond our current circumstances into the possibility of
    something new. The Christian tradition places a great deal of
    value on the role of resurrection. The belief that Jesus lived,
    died, and rose again is a basic tenet of my faith. The gos-
    pels tell stories of Jesus traveling and bringing back people
    from the dead. From the church mothers, I learned that the
    same creative spirit that allowed Jesus to perform his many
    miracles is present within us. Our job is to slow down long
    enough to pay attention to that which is yearning to be (re)
    born.

    Question: *What wants to emerge?*

3. ***Living*** **as a testament to the possibility of the present.**
    Understanding our lives through the lenses of death and res-
    urrection helps us to see the miracle of life. A favorite refrain
    from the church women of my childhood was to "just keep
    living." It was a declaration that change is the one thing
    that we can be sure of in our lives. They understood faith is
    not the absence of doubt, but rather *trust in the absence of
    certainty*. When we let go of our obsession with certainty,
    our attempts to exercise control over our future, or replay
    the mistakes of our past, we find ourselves better able to see
    miracles that are happening right now.

    Question: *What is already blooming beautifully in the world?*

These themes and questions have become mantras in my faith
journey. More than words, they are the prayers that I repeat

when I feel the cold and slow creep of hopelessness enter my psyche.

Love Letters of Radical Hope

It is the second lesson from the church women—the gift of imagination—that I find myself returning to time and again as I navigate the uncertain terrain that is American life in the early twenty-first century.

What a time to be alive! We are not the first, nor (God willing) shall we be the last group of human beings to live through an apocalypse. During my second semester of seminary, as I familiarized myself with ancient Greek as a way of reading the New Testament anew, I learned that the root of the word apocalypse means "to uncover." It just so happens that three decades of my life occurred alongside a cultural inflection point with some of the deepest and most explicit moments of uncovering in the last half-century.

In the United States, these moments of uncovering have largely occurred around the topics considered impolite for dinner conversation, including race, religion, politics, gender, and sexuality. Clearly there is a reckoning afoot. Those whose voices for the first two centuries of our country's history were largely ignored—women, people of color, migrants, religious minorities, and our LGBTQ siblings—are beginning to break through. The response to these changes has not been welcomed by all segments of our society. Indeed, some believe that uplifting the voices of others somehow silences their own. Rather than moving toward difference and seeing it as an asset to our lives, they see it as an existential threat to the thriving of our democracy.

We are at the beginning and the end—a birth and a death. What has become clear to me is that the crisis before us is deeper than any surface-level disagreements about public policy; but rather it is indeed a spiritual crisis over the identity of our country. When a wound has been inflicted, or in this case uncovered, we do not call those who caused the harm to fix it. Rather, we lean on the healers, like the church mothers of my childhood, to nurse us back to health. I am convinced that the healing we need and seek can be found within the genius of our communities if we simply pay attention.

In 2014, I founded Faith Matters Network, a womanist-led organization focused on equipping faith leaders, community organizers, and activists—modern day healers—with tools for connection, spiritual sustainability, and accompaniment. Our tagline, "Healing the Healers," speaks to our deep desire to care for those who are doing the important restorative work to heal our communities. We believe that care—for self, others, and community—is the fuel for transformative social movements. Over the past six years, we have worked alongside folks on the frontlines of these moments of apocalyptic transformation. They include rural pastors who directly challenge white nationalist groups in their hometowns, young organizers who fight for reforms in the criminal justice system, and activists who seek care after years of placing their bodies in harm's way.

The book that follows is an attempt to capture some of the lessons I have learned along the way through engaging in this work. It is a series of love letters to the people in my life—past, present, and future—who embody this legacy of radical hope in their very beings. Some are personal heroes who planted seeds that I harvested. Others are family members and mentors who taught me how to tend to the gardens before me. The final group are playground prophets—those who are coming after me—who will cultivate their own fields of dreams. They are people who continue to help shape me, inspire me, and push me to apply the arts of healing to the discipline of hope. *All are my beloveds.*

This book is also a narrative of my unfolding grief journey as a daughter coming to terms with the death of her beloved mother. My mama, Christine Bailey, was one of the finest church women I have known. Beautifully flawed, fun-loving, wise, and resilient, the way she lived her too short life was radical hope made manifest. She loved God, her family, and her community with all of herself. She died of metastatic breast cancer on May 7, 2016. I miss her every day.

I have found that addressing such tender topics requires a type of vulnerability that does not come naturally to me, so I am using an old form of the written word, letters, as a window into my own story and perhaps an entry point into some bigger questions about faith, community, belonging, and the future that so many of us are asking in this season. I chose the missive as my vehicle for sharing these lessons, in part because letters are personal. They are intimate. They have a way of making people feel special when they receive them. My wish is that you may find a bit of yourself in these letters, and that through my story you will find a pathway back to your own. Perhaps you will find the inspiration to write someone in your life who inspires you with their radical hope.

At the center of this work are those Black women who have shaped and guided me along the way—the elders that I aspire to be like and the young women who push me to be and do better. I learned at a young age that growing old is a gift and not a promise.

Sandra Bland did not get to become an old Black woman.

Breonna Taylor did not get to become an old Black woman.

Atatiana Jefferson did not get to become an old Black woman.

Aja Raquell Rhone-Spears did not get to become an old Black woman.

Oluwatoyin Salau did not get to become an old Black woman.

None of them made it to their thirty-fifth birthday. Each was the victim of violence and systems that were not designed to protect Black women nor see us as worthy of care. May this book be a blessing to their memories.

With tenderness,

Jennifer

May 2021

Memory: What Is Dying?

"I used to think it was my rememory. You know. Some things you forget. Other things you never do. But it's not. Places, places are still there. If a house burns down, it's gone, but the place—the picture of it—stays, and not just in my rememory, but out there, in the world. What I remember is a picture floating around out there outside my head. I mean, even if I don't think it, even if I die, the picture of what I did, or knew, or saw is still out there. Right in the place where it happened."

— Toni Morrison, *Beloved*

As She Lay Dying
Letter to Motherless Child

No, in all these things we are more than conquerors through him who loved us. For I am convinced that neither death nor life, neither angels nor demons, neither the present nor the future, nor any powers, neither height nor depth, nor anything else in all creation, will be able to separate us from the love of God that is in Christ Jesus our Lord.

Romans 8:37–39 (NIV)

*"Sometimes I feel like a motherless child
A long way from home, a long way from home"*

Negro Spiritual

Dear Beloved,

I know how badly it hurts. I am writing this letter to tell you that grief, when fully embraced, is a journey with no discernable end. It has hills and valleys.

When I was twenty-eight years old, my mama died after a fourteen-year battle with cancer. For much of my adolescence and young adulthood, the fear of death hovered like a looming fog that threatened to block my ability to see anything and anyone clearly. I always felt like I was just one text or phone call from receiving the most devastating news of my life.

Even so, I acknowledge I was one of the lucky ones. Not every parent-child relationship is defined by unconditional love. For nearly three decades, I knew what it was like to be loved in spite of my failures, misgivings, and mistakes. My mama was and remains my best friend and closest confidante. When I feel lost, I still call upon her spirit to accompany and guide me through, and she always, always answers. Even four years after her transition, there are still moments when I pick up the phone and dial her number to share my latest bit of news or gossip before realizing that she will not be on the other end.

I want to tell you about the last few months of my mother's life in hopes that it may alleviate some of the loneliness you may be feeling and help you on your path to healing. As she lay dying, writing became a sanctuary for me when words failed to take shape in my mouth. What follows are words written at her bedside during the last few months of her life.

* * *

Yesterday Mama told me she was afraid of dying. I listened carefully while lying next to her in the hospital bed we received from hospice. We placed the bed in the front room with the big picture window. Sometimes when the sun peeks through the lace curtains just right, her chocolate brown skin glows radiantly, highlighting the curves of her nose. It is the same nose I see every time I look in the mirror.

Growing up, this room was ornamental, not functional. The white couches were my mother's pride and joy, only to be sat upon on Christmas mornings or when entertaining honored guests. Over the past two months, this once uninhabited space has become a sanctuary for sharing secrets. Against the gentle murmur of her oxygen machine, we confess our deepest fears and greatest hopes. Yet this is the first time either of us has dared to speak the painful and obvious truth that lay before us: My mom may very well be Superwoman, but immortal she is not. Together, we cry.

When there are no words, tears may be the only prayers you can utter.

There are times during this period when Mama asks for my insights into the nature and will of God. It is a strange reminder of the multiple identities I inhabit even in the midst of this crisis. As a seminary-trained minister, I am supposed to be well versed in matters of death and dying. Yet no amount of training can prepare you for the moment when someone tells you that the most important person in your life has weeks to live. No class can teach you how to respond when your loved one grimaces in pain but cannot find the words to tell you how to help. When my own words escape me, and they often do, my default is to turn to scripture and read aloud from verses that sustained our kinfolk through the best and worst of times. They are messy, imperfect words situated in the text of a sacred book used by history to empower *and* destroy; to liberate *and* oppress.

My theology lives in the tension of the "and." I have not figured out just yet the relationship between the Christianity I practice, the politics I preach, the ethics I embody, and the Bible I read. The process of reconciling it all feels like a complicated routine of mental gymnastics full of twists, turns, and plenty of falls off of the balance beam. Yet, as I flip through the pages of Mama's Bible with its sticky notes and highlights, it is abundantly clear to me what her relationship is to the text. During the dark moments of her illness, in the midst of the chaos of chemo, the word of God is her light of hope. So, when we have conversations about things like forgiveness and the afterlife, I try to find the passages in her Bible with the most notes in the margins and pray God places on my lips the right thing to say, if just for today.

* * *

Before I was a clergywoman, I was the daughter of a sick mother. For as long as I can remember, my greatest fear was losing the one who gave me life. I learned about her cancer diagnosis on my fourteenth birthday. That morning my parents explained that Mama would be going into the hospital for a procedure called a lumpectomy to remove a tumor in her right breast. I cannot remember now whether I chose to stay home alone that day or if I did so at my parents' request. Trauma has a way of collapsing memories and nightmares into one. Sometime in the early afternoon my friend Colleen and her mom brought over a small round birthday cake, hoping to temper my shock. I had no idea that Mama was sick. During the preceding weeks I had been preoccupied with saying goodbye to the places and people that had defined my childhood, as I was preparing to leave and start high school in the big city. My dad accepted a position in his hometown of Chicago several months before. Rather than uprooting me in the middle of my eighth grade year, they decided that my mom and I would stay behind to allow me to finish the year surrounded by the landmarks of my childhood. Mama would stay behind for a few months longer to prepare the house for sale before joining us. The move would be a fresh start for our entire family.

A week after my mother's surgery, I would leave the bucolic beauty of my small town to start high school under the heat of Chicago's bright lights. Prior to my mother's diagnosis, the decision for me to leave had been an easy one for my parents. For all of its charms, my hometown was a difficult place for a little Black girl to grow up. It is a place that resists change in the name of tradition and where difference is a deficit rather than strength. In a community that was 90 percent white, my family stood out. I learned on the school playground that the politics of race is a messy and violent business.

Chicago was my escape hatch from a school system that chewed up and spit out Black kids from my community in juvenile courts and teenage pregnancy centers. Today the city is alive in the public imagination as an epicenter of urban violence. "Urban" being a code word for Black and violence applied as a catch-all phrase that emphasizes Black death at the hands of Black people rather than illuminating the systemic oppression that has brutalized and marginalized those same people for generations. For me, Chicago, with its gifted schools and cultural institutions, represented hope and opportunity. It never occurred to me that my liberation would come at the cost of leaving my mama behind.

While I begin to pick at the icing on my slice of birthday cake with a fork, my mom is being put under anesthesia for the first in a long series of surgeries and procedures. She carries that folded list in her wallet between her driver's license and her AAA membership card. She jokingly refers to it as a record of her missing body parts. Her uterus is gone. So is half of her thyroid. I know that she keeps it close for the same reason she keeps a memory book—dates and online passwords have not been as easy to remember since the cancer spread to her brain. The scars on her flesh tell the stories of organs removed and expectations delayed. Yet even now she rarely complains.

For the life of me I cannot figure out if that trait is a virtue or a hindrance. So often Black women are denied full access to our suffering. We are taught to suppress and bury it so that we can be of service to others, as if attending to the fullness of our own human experience is a vice. Our strength suffocates us. If anything, her yelps of pain today are a sign of just how frequently she concealed her hurt in the past. Then she could grin and bear it. Now she must rely on us to help relieve the sharp stabbing sensation in her abdomen where the cancer is spreading.

Fourteen and a half years later, I can still remember how sweet that birthday cake tasted. Sweetness is a trait that I have come to associate with sickness. Pills crushed in applesauce. Nutritional shakes consumed when nausea will not allow solid food to digest. The only things Mama wants to eat these days are ice cream and jelly beans.

As a child, her sweet tooth earned her the nickname Cookie. In my family, the granting of nicknames is a sacred business. They can often be more predictive of the course of a person's life journey than the name on their birth certificate. The story goes that, as a toddler, Aunt Doll would often keep my mama and her cousin Mae while their mothers were working. As Aunt Doll rolled out the dough for morning biscuits, Mama would stand up on a chair near the counter, helping spread the flour then pinching off tiny pieces of the dough and sticking them in her mouth. At a young age, she learned that the delicious parts of life do not come without preparation and work. To this day, thanks to Aunt Dolly, more people call Mama Cookie than her given name Christine.

We brought Mama home from the hospital for the last time on February 23, four days before her sixty-third birthday. That morning the doctors had said there was nothing they could do to stop the fluid from building on her lungs, so Mama demanded we bring her home. Black mothers are willful creatures. Stand in their way and there is usually hell to pay. Her decision was not a surrender, but a declaration of independence. No more poison being pumped into her body once a week. No more doctors probing or nurses poking. No more hospital rooms. She decided that her God, her body, and her desire to live would guide the path ahead of her. She has been in the front room ever since.

I'd never felt the full weight of what it means to be an only child before these past few months. The night Mama began hospice care I'd dreamt that our family home had been moved off of its foundation. Like a dollhouse, the rooms remained intact. The daily routines of life continued. Yet, the illusion of privacy was shattered as the most intimate parts of our lives were exposed and laid bare for public consumption. I awoke, knowing in my gut that everything had changed. My mom is the solid ground upon which our family unit was built. Her body is now telling her that it can no longer hold the heaviness alone.

With deep gratitude, I have seen my family and community show up for us. Her first week home things looked bleak. She moved in and out of responsiveness and the hospice nurse told us to prepare for the worst. Within forty-eight hours, my chosen and biological family flew in from around the country to accompany us. Those who could not come sent care packages, kind notes, and made phone calls just to check in. Granny comes to stay for weeks on end to take care of her baby girl. She gets very little sleep when she is here and refuses to sleep anywhere but on the couch beside Mama's bed.

When the rooms are empty and I am alone with my thoughts, exhaustion sets in. This is the first time since I left home for college that I have lived with my parents for an extended period of time. When I am weak, my humanity starts to show and I long for my life back. I want to drink wine with my roommate and plot our paths to take the world by storm. I want to go on dates with my fiancé and do the mundane daily tasks that will be the cornerstone of our life together. I want to make plans with my friends that I can actually keep. Most of all, I want to call my mom and tell her all the silly things about my day. I want her to be healthy and well. I want things to be *normal again*.

When I snap out of it, I remember that this image of normalcy is a fantasy. Mama has been sick for half of my life. Until now, it has been easy to ignore that reality. We flourished as a family unit because of her determination to beat cancer by living. As my play auntie Deborah says, "She teaches us how to fight." Her friends tell stories of her showing up to help them plan events minutes after completing a chemo treatment. During the yearly moves that became a hallmark of my twenties, she was always right there with me—Chicago, Nashville, New York, and Washington, D.C.— helping me pick out furniture and art to make each temporary home my own.

I have no doubt that my mama will fight until the day her and her God agree it is time for her to join the ancestors. Sometimes that fight will be physical and at other times it will be spiritual. This one thing I know to be true: I am blessed to have a mother who loves me and whom I love. That is a gift I will never take for granted. It is a gift worth the price of placing everything else in my life on hold to accompany her at this stage of her journey. So, until the time comes for us to say our final goodbye, I will lay beside her sharing secrets, eating jelly beans, and being present for her as she has always been present for me.

* * *

She died on Mother's Day eve at 9:32 a.m. The sun was pouring through the lace curtains surrounding the big picture window, illuminating her chocolate skin as it always had. Granny had stepped out of the room to take a telephone call. It was just Mama and me. I put my head on her chest so that I could hear her heartbeat. The nurse told me that hearing was one of the last senses to go. So, during the pauses between her last few labored breaths, I whispered "I love you" into her ear. She took in one last gasp of air and the beating stopped.[5]

She seemed at peace when she died. Her face had an eerie calm about it. Her mouth was slightly ajar, but the muscles in her face were relaxed. Someone suggested that we open the window so that her spirit could be free to return to God. When I was little, I told Mama that the beams of sunlight that peak through the clouds on a perfect day were escalators ascending to heaven. The thickness of her presence in the house in the days that followed made me think that she was in no hurry to make her way up that rotating staircase just yet. I think she knew how much we needed to feel close to her. Granny went home the day after she passed to spend some time alone with her sorrow before the funeral. Daddy was too immobilized by heartbreak to do anything but keep himself busy and clean the house. It was left to me to make the arrangements for our celebration of Mama's life.

The days following the death of a loved one are a chaotic dance of making plans and managing expectations. Decisions must be made quickly and with authority, lest they become the casualty to an unending stream of unsolicited feedback. The boldness with which people freely express their opinions to the bereaved is astounding. It is inevitable that the voices of those who were least heard in the final days speak the loudest; their performance of grief is the most theatrical. I took many long drives the week after Mama's death so that I could shout at the top of my lungs what I could not utter in the face of family members and well-meaning church folk.

---

[5] Jennifer Bailey, "The Political Nature of Balck Women's Trauma," *Sojourners*, May 12, 2017 https://sojo.net/articles/political-nature-black-women-s-trauma, Accessed June 28, 2021.

When I decided to preach her eulogy, there were whispers. They were divided into two camps. Those who were genuinely worried about my well-being and those who simply thought I was not capable of doing it. As a clergywoman, one of the first things you learn is how to sniff out the putrid stench of sexism from the pews. Most often, it attempts to coat itself in flowery language and sweet gestures of false concern. In the case of Mama's eulogy their words sounded something like:

> "You wouldn't want to be too emotional and take the focus off of your mom."
>
> "Are you sure that you are strong enough? I don't know if you are strong enough and there is no shame in that."
>
> "You and your mom were so close, so why don't you let one of the [male] preachers speak words of comfort over you?"

The message behind their coded words was clear: "Leave this task to the men, little girl." Despite the resistance, I had the sense that delivering Mama's eulogy would be one of the most important things I would do in my life. It was. Here is what I said:

> I had the opportunity to walk alongside my mom these past three months, in the final stretch of her journey. It was the greatest gift of my life. In the process, the words of Stuart Scott have echoed in my mind, "You beat cancer by how you live."
>
> My mama lived with grace, resilience, and courage, and in the process taught us all how to fight. I am because she was. Like so many Black women, her back was strong from carrying so

much weight and so many people. It is a reality I both lament and celebrate—a bittersweet reminder that for some women strength is not an option, but it is a necessity for our survival.

And what of God? What of the promise of the afterlife? I must confess that Christian tropes about her being in a better place provide minimal comfort in this moment. I have no doubt they are true. I can feel her presence even as her spirit has transitioned into its next phase. I know she is surrounded by the love of the saints who have preceded her in death. I am sure that Uncle Phil, Aunt Doll, and Auntie Belinda are helping her into her long white robe. I'd like to think that my dear friend Josephine is excitedly showing her around heaven. Yet, the words of my tradition in which I find the greatest comfort are these two: Jesus wept. It is a reminder that my savior mourns alongside those who mourn; that grief and lament are part of the process.

I will miss my mom every day of my life. I will miss the contours of her face, the creases of her smile, and the furrow of her brow when she was displeased. I will miss her laugh, which was neither polite nor restrained, but bold and loud. I will miss her cube steaks and gravy. I will miss her phone greeting of "Hi, My Baby." I will miss the excitement of her voice when she found a deal on sale. I will miss standing next to her in worship as she uttered the tongues of angels and unapologetically worshipped her God. I will miss sharing secrets. I will miss her smell, which I find myself searching for in blankets that adorned her hospice bed.

I am hurting. It is a pain that pierces the very depths of my self-understanding because I have not known a world without her. Yet, in my hurt I also rejoice, for she is no longer in pain. I feel grateful for friends, family, and community that surround me, lift me up, and love me hard.

Be at rest, my mama. It is time for God to enjoy you.

* * *

Today, beloved, I am still searching for peace that alludes me. There are so many conversations that I wish that I'd summoned the courage to initiate in those last few months. Lingering questions about Mama's own journey into womanhood, lessons she learned along the way, or things that she regretted. Instead, I spent my time feeling—feeling overwhelmed, feeling confused, feeling my heart break and remake itself over and over again. Even as time propels me forward, the past keeps pulling me back. When I close my eyes, I can see her last few breaths. I feel her last heartbeat.

In her 1993 Nobel Prize acceptance speech, the great Toni Morrison reminded us that, "We die. That may be the meaning of life."

I have found that death is a misunderstood teacher. Her methods are harsh and definitive. Yet, as the years have transpired, I have found her to be one of the most consistent and compassionate instructors of my life. Her lessons have taught me how to value life *and* not to hold onto it too tightly.

So as you continue down the road of grief, remember that the path you are treading is one that is unique to you. Nobody can tell you how long it will be or the shape it will take. What I do know is that, if you are open, it can and will transform you for the better.

Love,

Cookie's Baby Girl

Who Will Take Care of My Baby?

A Letter to MarShawn and Those Contemplating Suicide

On February 8, 2016, award-winning activist, poet, and community organizer MarShawn McCarrel II committed suicide on the steps of the Ohio Statehouse. He was 23 years old.

Dear Beloved,

I've never met you, but ever since I learned a bit about your story—as a poet, activist, and community organizer—you have not escaped my mind. Like you, I grew up a Black child in flyover country, the place where thistle and dandelions seep through the cracks of abandoned factories and broken promises. My ancestors migrated here fleeing the daily terror of life in the agrarian South, where Black bodies were still seen as chattel and the cry of Baby Suggs, Holy, that "we flesh, we flesh"[6] fell upon ears that refused to hear.

Emancipation brought a fleeting freedom. We were no longer property, yet our bodies were still not our own. Reconstruction unleashed the fresh fury of white Southerners whose cities and fields were left covered in a soot of defeat. From the ashes, they began building a new social construct with the vestiges of the

---

[6] Toni Morrison, *Beloved* (New York: First Vintage International Edition, 2004), 103.

plantation system. Paramilitary groups in red shirts and white hoods terrorized the countryside, burning Black homes and threatening the lives of any who questioned white authority. When the last of the federal troops returned on horseback to their homes in the North, they passed laws separating public facilities and limiting access to the ballot box for our kinfolk.

We were no longer slaves, but sharecroppers—still bound to the land and caught up in a cycle of exploitation and abuse. Gone was the whip of the overseer. In its place were chains of debt that bound us to the owners of the land. For decades, we tilled the blood-soaked soil, coaxing life out of the dirt and growing crops that would feed and clothe the world.

Then they started killing us for fun.

They wrapped ropes around our necks and hoisted us in magnolia trees. Our Black and Brown bodies left swaying in the sweltering heat for public consumption. The Equal Justice Initiative in Montgomery, Alabama, names 4,400 victims of "racial terror lynchings" in twelve Southern states from 1877 to 1950.[7] Many victims were murdered without being accused of any crime, for minor social transgressions, or for demanding basic rights.[8]

So our peoples boarded buses and trains and followed the North Star in search of a better life. What they found were urban ghettos and the same horrors of racism sung to a different tune. Your people landed in Ohio. Mine in Illinois.

MarShawn, your friends say that you wanted something for the world that the world wasn't ready to receive—peace and unity. In

---

[7] Equal Justice Initiative, *Lynching in America: Confronting the Legacy of Racial Terror* (3d Ed., 2017), https://lynchinginamerica.eji.org/report.

[8] Jennifer Bailey, "Strange Fruit of a Different Name", *The Huffington Post,* April 29, 2015, Updated June 29, 2019, https://www.huffpost.com/entry/strange-fruit-of-a-different-name_b_7163030. Accessed June 28, 2021.

interviews you said you needed a pistol that shoots hope so you could light the hood up, and light it up you did—with art, with poetry, and with activism. So you founded Pursuing Our Dreams in 2013 to feed the homeless—not out of a sense of charity, altruism, or messianic complex, but because you knew firsthand what it was like to not know where you would lay your head at the end of the night.

When Mike Brown was crucified on an altar of pavement, laid bare for the world to see the brutality inflicted upon Black and Brown bodies, you answered the call. Alongside your brothers, sisters, and siblings in the Ohio Student Association, you organized for justice for Mike and John Crawford and Tamir Rice—a baby assassinated for the crime of playing on a playground.

Everyone was so blinded by the brightness of your star that they could not clearly see the darkness that surrounded it. No one does. They saw the awards, the red carpets, and the résumé, but they did not see you. They could not see the heaviness you were carrying, the weight of death placed on your back.

You said on Facebook that your demons won that day—so you placed steel to temple and pulled the trigger, finally free from the pain that enveloped you. Your lifeless body remained on the steps of the Ohio Statehouse as your spirit was finally free from a specific pain I will never know.

I am writing this eulogy for you so that you know even now that you are not alone. I too have felt the constant companion of depression. A few days before you died, my mother went into the hospital for the last time. I had the honor of journeying alongside her as she took her final walk toward death after a fourteen-year battle with cancer. Before we knew the path we were on, before the word hospice entered our vocabulary, when we thought her hospital visit was just a temporary one—we had time.

One day, as we sat in her hospital room enjoying a rare glimpse of the winter sun peeking through the blinds, my mama turned to me and told me a story I had never heard. I cannot remember clearly what prompted it, but I imagine after three weeks in a hospital bed, death was at the forefront of her mind. Her story began not long after the miscarriage that would have brought my baby brother into the world. I had not reached kindergarten yet and did not have a clear understanding of what was going on at the time. I just knew that one day I was going to be a big sister and the next, mommy was extremely sad.

In a moment of quiet despair, she told me she placed her foot on the accelerator and began to drive down the boat launch ramp into the murky mud-tinged waters of the Mississippi River. As the wheels became as wet as her tear-stained cheeks, she said she heard a voice ask, "Who will take care of your baby?" meaning me. So she placed the car in reverse and drove home.

That day my mother chose to live for me. It was a sentiment I recognized because at age fourteen I chose to live for her. It was just a few months after my move to Chicago. As a child, I had spent summers in the city with my grandparents, so I was familiar with its rhythms. My mom had stayed behind in my hometown to receive the first of many rounds of treatment for her cancer diagnosis. The plan was that she would move up when she was healthy. So I learned how to exist outside the daily grounding of my mother's presence. I shared space with my dad in Chicago, but mostly I missed my former life. My dad's attempt to balance the growing responsibilities of his new job and sick wife meant there was little space for much else. Gradually, I began to sink into myself. I stopped eating. I did not speak at school. I worried about my mom all the time. I spent hours on instant messenger talking to my friends who were now 325 miles away. I had never felt so alone.

One day after an argument with my dad, I grabbed a pair of scissors from my desk and held them to my wrist. Applying a bit of pressure, I imagined the relief I would feel if everything would just go away. Then a refrain entered my mind, "Mommy would be sad. Mommy would be sad." The thought of my mother crying for me while hooked up to a chemotherapy machine was too much for me to handle. So I dropped the scissors and called my best friend instead.

* * *

As you journey to the great beyond, be sure to send my love to my friends Nina and Jo. In the first three decades of my life, seven of my friends — all women of color — shared the stories of their suicide attempts with me. The origin of their pain was particular, but there were familiar echoes in each story. There were feelings of isolation and loneliness. The burden of never believing you will be enough. Shame and secrets passed down like family heirlooms casting their shadows from one generation to the next. Abuse, neglect, rejection, erasure ... all deeply felt but rarely vocalized out of a fear that their pain did not deserve to be heard and shared.

Seven women, seven stories. Only Nina and Jo's ended with obituaries.

Nina and I met in Mrs. Biel's English class not long after my move to Chicago. Her fierce intellect and wit were her superpowers. Sometimes it felt like she could stop time with her thoughtful questions and force those around her to think more deeply about the topic at hand. She wore her natural hair in two-strand twists before it was popular to do so, and whenever she was lost in thought she would twirl her index finger around a piece of her hair as if the answer she was looking for could be found in that particular strand.

It was Nina who took me to my first H20 Bible Club meeting after school. I told her that I was a Christian but had not found a church in town to call my own just yet. So she pressed in her gentle way for me to come along. She always had a way of pushing people outside of their comfort zones with love. It's like even as a teenager she could see the potential for great things in us, even when we could not see them in ourselves. That first Bible study was a lifeline that helped sustain me in the midst of my darkness. It was a light of possibility when I could not see a way forward.

I don't remember the last time we spoke. I think it was a couple years after we'd graduated from college. Nina was on her way to the best law school in the country. I remember the conversation being sweet and brief. I had finally decided to stop running from my call to ministry and was going to divinity school. My pathway to ministry was not linear.

I regret that I did not think to thank her for helping me see God when my faith was shaken by my mother's first tussle with cancer. It was my introduction to the spiritual wilderness of doubt, a place where I would in later years pitch my tent often in the midst of my search for meaning. The memories of these Bible studies have become fuzzy around the edges. I cannot recall a single scripture passage we explored. Yet, my body remembers what it was like to be held in the midst of questions by my friends. Nina's hugs of encouragement will forever be imprinted on me.

Nina seemed to be searching for something in that last conversation. I could not tell just what. I did not suspect that thing might lead to her leaving us. I found out about her death when I was on a trip abroad. I was sitting in a dorm room in Southern India when I received an email from a mutual high school friend informing me of the news. My breath stopped. My first thought was how *courageous and cowardly* her death seemed to me. I still wince when I think of it. I feel ashamed of how quickly I rushed to judgment rather than hold her with the same compassion that she always held me.

But I was younger then. I did not have the experience or maturity to hold complexity when considering the circumstances surrounding her death. I was looking to assign blame as a means to understand. What I now know is that my job was not to understand but to feel the weight of her loss. It is still heavy. I suspect it will always be. Yet when I allow myself to feel it, I am reminded of my deep love for her. I am reminded that the tears are a prelude to a smile as I remember her back into being.

Nina's death took my breath away. Jo's death crushed my heart. She was one of my best friends and I have missed her every day since. I met Jo on an evening when the heavens painted the barren trees with a fresh coat of white snow. It was December 2005, and we were rapidly approaching the end of our first semester of college. With the thoughts of finals turning knots in my stomach, I knew I needed to get away from the uncaring eyes of my textbooks and the unforgiving hand of the clock ticking closer and closer to my first exam. My escape came in the form of a meet and greet with fellow freshman handpicked to participate in a three-year public service program. Over the course of our college experience we would volunteer with nonprofit organizations in the communities surrounding campus working on issues from environmental justice to domestic violence and build bridges with our neighbors to the north, south, and east.

As I grabbed a slice of pizza from the box, my eyes drifted in the direction of a woman sitting on the opposite side of the room. When I took the seat next to her, I could not know that I was meeting a sister with whom I would share secrets, totally-worth-it gourmet meals out of my price range that forced me to eat ramen noodles for weeks, wild nights dancing until our feet started to blister, and, most of all, jazz. I had never met another nineteen-year-old who shared my affinity for bebop and the soulful, imperfect voice of Nina Simone. For the next four years, we found ourselves in smoky jazz lounges, sophisticated oak bars, and back-alley concert venues listening to the music swing. We graduated, but our love for one another and music would continue as the beat marched on.

Three months before she died, she came to visit me in Nashville before moving back home to Hong Kong for six months. It felt like old times. We shared secrets in our pajamas, posed for fancy pictures that we staged, and took a road trip to Bourbon Trail where we gorged ourselves on bacon and booze. It was perfect. When I got the call about her death, I could not help thinking that perhaps she had been on a goodbye tour. Her picture sits on the bookshelf behind my desk, a reminder that her presence is near and she always has my back.

* * *

Marshawn, you were neither the first nor the last young activist to die under mysterious and tragic circumstances in recent years. In Ferguson, there were six in four years. Deandre Joshua and Darren Seals were found inside torched vehicles, both having been shot in the head. Three others died of apparent suicides. Bassem Masri collapsed on a bus, his death ruled an overdose. So far in Louisville there have been two since Breonna passed. Their lives are emblematic of the fatal price our protest can exact when we become so preoccupied with the strategy and tactics of our movements for justice and we fail to see and honor the humanity of those pushing them forward.

There is something about the sorrow of Black folks that over-whelms and envelopes. We carry in our DNA the stories of people who will never be named or known. Their lives were reduced to labor in service of a nation whose response to us was always violent. Even our joy has tinges of sadness because in that joy we remember where we have been. We name the trauma experienced by our kindred and celebrate our resilience. I have no doubt that you could bounce back from adversity with the best. Your story tells me as much. But even the strongest bridge eventually begins to crack under pressure.

They say that suicide is a permanent solution to a temporary problem. What happens when the problems ahead of you are not momentary, but endemic to the society in which you live? For people of color in this country, our trauma is by nature political. Our very embodiment places us in a never-ending cycle of entanglement with systems, people, and policies designed to perpetuate violence and domination. This is a reality you knew too well. Your work fighting for the liberation of Black people and demanding an end to police brutality put you in constant encounter with the carelessness with which systems designed to "protect and serve" treat Black life.

A little piece of each of us dies with each viral video of unarmed Black bodies being shot and killed over the past few years. Perhaps it was the willingness of others to share and spread these documents of death that was most troubling. Unjustified killings should never be entertainment. Yet, we cannot turn away. Around the corner there is always someone else. Someone who belonged to a family, belonged to friends, belonged to a community that loved them. It is too much for me. I imagine it was too much for you as well.

The work of generative somatics teaches us that trauma is both an individual and collective experience that is held in our bodies. Everyday experiences of racism, classism, and sexism often show up in the form of stress, mental illness, and disease. Research shows that chronic stress can disrupt metabolic, vascular, and immune systems and cause cells to age quicker. It suggests that Black Americans' health deteriorates more rapidly than other groups' because we bear a heavier stress load.[9]

Because our trauma is political, our healing must be as well. It is not adjacent to our cries for justice. Healing *is* the work of justice. People of color engaging in the act of loving themselves, fully, in a society that deems them disposable is indeed both countercultural and revolutionary.

One of the great lies of our American culture is that rugged individualism is the highest form of self-expression. Politicized healing looks like creating brave spaces to see and be seen, to hear and be heard. Spaces to surface the trauma that we carry and to uncover the strength that can be found in our vulnerability. It is work that cannot be done in isolation and must be held in community with others.

MarShawn, I hope you have found your healing. If angels do indeed have wings, I pray they wrap them around you and give you the sense of peace and unity you never found here.

Love,

A Fellow Sister in the Struggle

[9] Jennifer Bailey, "The Political Nature of Balck Women's Trauma," *Sojourners*, May 12, 2017 https://sojo.net/articles/political-nature-black-women-s-trauma, Accessed June 28, 2021.

Naming the Lost

A Letter of Communal Lament

This is what the Lord Almighty says: "Consider now! Call for the wailing women to come; send for the most skillful of them. Let them come quickly and wail over us till our eyes overflow with tears and water streams from our eyelids. The sound of wailing is heard from Zion: "How ruined we are! How great is our shame! We must leave our land because our houses are in ruins." Now, you women, hear the word of the Lord; open your ears to the words of his mouth. Teach your daughters how to wail; teach one another a lament. Death has climbed in through our windows and has entered our fortresses; it has removed the children from the streets and the young men from the public squares.

Jeremiah 9:17-21 (NIV)

Dear Beloved,

Can you hear the wailing women beckoning us to prayer?

If you pause long enough, you can hear their cries calling out in their mother tongues from rural villages and suburban hospitals, at gravesites and funeral pyres, lamenting those lives lost during the coronavirus pandemic. Sisters, daughters, aunts, neighbors, and friends.

My chosen sister, Micky, is one of those wailing women. She lost her mother, Janet, in the early days of the pandemic in the United States. When Ms. Howard first started experiencing symptoms, we did not fully grasp how the disease impacted the body, especially not the bodies of Black women. When the shortness of breath and chest pains began, the doctors diagnosed her with congestive heart failure and sent her home with a few new medications. A few short weeks later she was on a respirator.

Abba Kyari, Abdelfattah Abdrabbo, Abraham Candelaria, Abrar Ahmad Malik, Abrar Ahmad Malik, Adrian Baker, Agustina Gutierrez, Al Phillips, Alan Abel, Alan Leif Lund, Alan Twofoot, Albert Johnson Trousdale, Albert Stokes Sr., Alberto Castro, Alex Hsu, Alexander J. Glodkowski, Alfred Buchetto, Alfredo Plaza Ramirez, Ali Dennis Guillermo, Alice Coopersmith Furst, Alice Pollock, Alton Townsel, Alvin Elton, Alyce Gullattee, Amelia Michels, Amil Padezanin ...

Accompanying Micky during her mother's illness, I became reacquainted with a part of my identity that I thought I buried with my mama: the daughter of a sick mother. The checklists of questions, obscure medical terminology, and tips for how to befriend the nurse on duty all came flooding back like muscle memory. As quarantine began in earnest, I tried to share as best I could the knowledge I had acquired over the years. Somehow it still seemed insufficient.

Cancer is a recognizable foe with reliable patterns and progression. There are thousands of support groups and websites dedicated to empowering families to the best and most informed decisions possible. I could sit by my mother's bedside. Micky could not. At the time, COVID-19 was an unknown enemy as lethal as it was mysterious. We still were trying to understand how the disease was transmitted. There was no clear treatment regime, only experimental drug regimens that lacked clinical evidence.

So, Micky took to social media to gather information from healthcare professionals treating the disease in real time. She shared her mother's unfolding story in hopes of finding others who were providing care for the loved ones with similar symptoms. She shot down trolls and armchair physicians declaring the disease a hoax. She did everything she could to be an informed, loving, and fierce advocate for her mom's care.

Janet Howard died on April 14, 2020. She was seventy-one years old.

… Aminaindalif (pronounced: "uh-meen-duh-in-dalif") Trisha, Andre Ferguson, André Steadman, Andrea Circle Bear, Andrew DiMaggio, Angel Escamilla, Angela Faith White, Angela White, Anne Martinez, Anne Mary Gagne, Annette (Fratturo) Possidento, Annie Glenn, Annie Grant, Annis Creese, Anthony Larry Rush, Anthony Velez, Antoinette "Annette" Meyer, Antoinette Lutz, Antonio Aviles, Antonio Nieves, Antonio Solomon, April Dunn, Araceli Buendia Ilagan …

Not long after Mrs. Howard's death, my colleague Margaret reminded me of the story of the wailing women in the book of Jeremiah.[10] It is the story of a displaced people exiled from their homeland. Death looms large as a character who creeps through the windows of unsuspecting homes, taking with him children and those in the prime of their lives. God tells the people to call on the keeners, women skilled in the art of collective grief, to teach them how to mourn.

Why? Because the act of public lamentation is therapeutic. There are times the weight of loss is too heavy to carry alone, so the only suitable response to the horrors of the world is to

---

[10] Margaret Ernst, "God, the Keening Woman: Wailing the Lost," *Unbound: An Interactive Journal of Christian Social Justice* (May 2020), https://justiceunbound.org/god-the-keening-woman-wailing-the-lost.

weep, yell, and rage in community.[11] The wailing women of Judah used their gifts to help their people acknowledge and process the trauma they carried and point them down the path of healing. Their work was essential.

... Araceli Buendia Ilagan, Arlene Saunders, Arlola Rawls, Arnold Budish, Aron Jordan, Art Whistler, Arthur Forte, Arthur Freiman, Arthur Friedman, Arturo Millan, Asela Gejo, Audelia MacGregor, Aymer Morera, Azalea Bates, Baldwin Domingo, Barbara Ann Ryan, Barbara Soroff, Barbara Wilding, Beatrice Eisemann (pronounced: eyes-man), Beirish Berger, Ben Luderer, Ben Schaeffer, Benigno Perez Jr., Benjamin Bush Jr., Bernabel "Pepe" Serrano Mena, Bernard David "Bernie" Seckler, Bernard Michael Goddard, Bernardo Gonzalez, Bernie Freedman, Bernie Juskiewicz, Bertha Mae Reddic, Berton Sumner Fliegel, Bettie Traxler, Betty Jo Clark, Betty Leskela Palma, Betty Lou (Jacobsen) Foster-Workman, Beverly Glass, Beverly Holloway Reep, Beverly June Collins, Beverly Reep, Bill Chambers, Bill Mantell, Bill Tighe, Billy, Billy Birmingham, Billy Leroy "Bill" Smith, Binyomin Abramowitz, Blanche Johnson, Bob Barnum, Bob Dema, Bobby Joseph Hebert Sr., Bobby Lee Barber ...

On May 21, 2020, Micky read her mother's name aloud as part of #NamingTheLost, an online vigil honoring those who died of COVID-19. Over the course of 1,440 minutes, we read one thousand names. One thousand names. One thousand lives. They were friends and lovers. They were musicians, construction workers, nurses, doctors, painters, short-order cooks, PTA members, street hustlers, teachers, preachers, and so much more. At the time of the vigil, just more than 100,000 people in

---

[11] L. Juliana M. Claassens, "Calling the Keeners: The Image of the Wailing Woman As Symbol of Survival in a Traumatized World," *Journal of Feminist Studies in Religion*. Vol. 26, No. 1, Special Introduction from the Religion and Politics Editor (Spring 2010), 63-77.

the United States had died as a result of the novel coronavirus. As I am writing to you, the global number of deaths is now in the millions.

When the pandemic began, so many of us struggled to comprehend the level of devastation and death wreaking havoc on families across the nation. Some averted their eyes, denying the severity of the crisis and finding consolation in modern-day snake oil salesmen peddling conspiracy theories and pseudo-science. Yet, for those whose lives found them at the epicenter of the plague, either because of where they lived or the color of their skin, it was clear that life would never be the same. The ringing of church bells became indistinguishable from the sound of sirens. Each symbolizing the arrival of the angel of death once more.

... *Bobby Pin, Bobby Wilkerson, Brandel "Brandi" Steif, Bredy Pierre-Louis, Brenda Perryman, Brian Axsmith, Brian Callagan, Brian Holcomb, Brian R. Miller, Brittany Bruner-Ringo, Bruce Edward Davis, Bruce Elder Anderson, Bryson Kent Bowman, Burton "Bud" Rose, Caitlin Whisnant, Caleb Saint Surin, Callie Roundtree, Calvin Richardson, Capt. Doug Hickok, Captain Franklin Williams, Carl Donald Brewster, Carl Pitaro, Carl Redd, Carl White, Carla Thompson, Carlene Edwards, Carlos Calderon, Carlos DeLeon, Carol DeWitt, Carol Jean Carpenter Brock, Carol Lee Taylor ...*

It did not have to be this way.

More deafening than the clarion call of ancestors beckoning so many people home to their gods was the silence of "leaders" who valued poll numbers more than people's anguish. In their effort to obfuscate the dire straits before us, they lied. They hid. They downplayed. They deflected.

The consequences were innumerable. Who knows how many lives might have been spared had they just opened their eyes and believed what they saw? One of the more insidious ramifications of their inaction is that it denied us the opportunity to mourn collectively as a nation united in our heartbreak. There comes a point in all our grief journeys where the words, "I am so sorry for your loss," begin to ring hollow. People are trained to say these words because it feels like the right or appropriate thing to do. They are platitudes, lacking substance, that allow us to distance ourselves from the suffering of others.

There are terms for this type of emotional distancing, "psychic numbing," "compassion fatigue," and "spiritual bypassing" to name a few.[12] Though each is unique, they all point to a common sociological phenomenon. When the number of victims of a tragedy increases, our empathy reliably decreases. It is true of natural disasters. It is true of famine. It is even true of genocide. Our brains are not predisposed to absorb the extent of human suffering these calamities represent. We care a great deal when a person is at risk, particularly a person that we know. Yet, against the backdrop of mass atrocity the importance of a single life begins to fade.

… Carol R. Petit, Carolann Christine Gann, Carole Brookins, Carole Rae Woodmansee, Carolyn Johnson, Carolyn Martins-Reitz, Carolyn Johnson, Carrie Ellen Lewis, Catherine MacDonald, Catherine Phillips-Russ, Cathy Drouin, Celia Marcos, Celia Po, Celia Yap Banago, Chad Capule, Chandra Montgomery, Charles "Duffy" Jernigan, Charles Canaan, Charles Connolly, Charles Edward "Skip" Adams III, Charles Hanberry, Charles Johnson, Charles Miles, Charles Powers, Charles Roberts, Charlie Safley, Chianti Jackson Harpool, Chris Firlit, Christine Mandegarian, Christine

---

[12] Paul Slovic, et.al, "Psychic Numbing and Mass Atrocity" (April 2011). In E. Shafir (Ed.), The behavioral foundations of public policy (126–142). *NJ: Princeton University Press*, 2013. *NYU School of Law, Public Law Research Paper* No. 11-56, Available at SSRN: https://ssrn.com/abstract=1809951

McLaurin, Christopher D. Loche, Christopher George "Chris" Firlit, Christopher W. Segura, Claborn Callens, Clair "Toby" Dunlap, Clair Marie Fuqua, Clara Lee Williams, Clarence Jackson Ballew, Clarence Lewis Sr., Claretha Boatman, Claudia Shirley, Claudia Teresa (Connolly) Johnson, Clifton Dougherty, Coby "Terrell" Adolph, Cody Lyster, Connie Sylene Hendrickson Thompson, Conrad C. Buchanan Jr., Conrad Duncker, Cornelius "Moose" Lawyer, Cornelius Frederick, Cornell Lamar "Dickey" Charles, Curtis Pearson, Curwin King, Cynthia "Chia" Mendoza, Cynthia Lee Segal, Dae Kwun Yoon ...

We are not a country that remembers well. Ask the typical American citizen about the origins of Memorial Day, and it's quite likely they will stare at you blankly. What has become a weekend to celebrate the unofficial beginning of summer with barbecues and trips to the beach began as a way to honor soldiers who died during the bloodiest conflict in American history—the American Civil War. Legend has it that the first of these celebrations took place in Charleston, South Carolina, a few months after the surrender of the Confederacy. A crowd of 10,000 people, mostly formerly enslaved persons, descended upon a country club that served as a prison for Union soldiers during the war. They staged a parade, recited Bible verse, carried bouquets to honor the dead, and sang "John Brown's Body"—a hymn dedicated to the militant abolitionist whose commitment to emancipation would serve as a kindling for the war.

For a moment, they suspended time and created a living monument to the collective memory of those gathered. For the first time, folks who once were chattels could openly weep for those they had lost to the institution that declared them three-fifths of a human being. They celebrated the overthrowing of principalities and powers that would rather see them dead than free. They survived against all odds and efforts to the contrary. They lived to tell their stories. Out of a bloody war, out of their grief and pain, they created a sacred space of joy.[13]

... Dalis Ramonas, Daniel Moran, Daniel Spector, Danielle Dicenso, Dar'yana Dyson, Darlene Kimball, Darren Edwards, Darrin Arriens, Dave Edwards, Dave Greenfield, David Boe, David C. Driskell, David Coveney, David Halter, David Michael Domina, David Sweeting, David Veloz, David Vidal, Deborah Hickey, Deborah Joseph-Saunders, Dee Pace, Delores Dacosta Thomas, Denis Vincent, Denise Larose, Denise Millet, Dennis Barrett, Dennis Bello, Dennis Dickson, Dennis Peters, Deon M. Crowell, Devin Dale Francis, Dez-Ann Romain, Diana T. Jun, Diana Tennant, Diane A. Jasmine, Diane Campbell, Diane Ramonas, Diane Simons, Dick Lucas, Dieugrand Nazaire, Dieumene Etienne, Dolores McGoldrick, Dolores Mena, Donald Fregelette, Donald Pijanowski, Donald Reed Herring, Donald Spitko, Dondrew Gibbons, Donnell Kirchner, Doris Bitner, Doris Brown, Doris Larmore, Doris Mathias, Dorothy Brunetti, Dorothy Jean "Dolly" Hart, Dorothy McGirt, Dorothy V. Indeck, Douglas Lambrecht, Earl Dave Bailey, Eastern Stewart Jr., Ed Siegel, Eddie Johnson Jr., Eddie Lee Hunter, Edie Morello, Edith Richemond, Edna Adams, Edna Daddario, Eduardo A. Piedra, Edward Jasmine Sr., Edward Singleton, Eileen Atkins, Elaine L. (McNeil) Moran, Elfriede H. Von Holtz, Elinor Downs, Elizabeth Anne Neill, Elizabeth Cota, Elizabeth Eugenia Wells, Elizabeth Lombardi, Ella King Russell Torrey, Ellen Rebecca Cummings, Ellie Gilbertson Smith, Ellis Marsalis, Eloise Rose Mast, Elton Washington ...

In the absence of a public space to grieve the tragic loss of life due to the coronavirus, our motley crew became modern-day wailing women and worked together to create a virtual homego-

---

[13] David Roos, "One of the Earliest Memorial Day Ceremonies was Held by Freed African Americans," *The History Channel,* May 24, 2019, Updated May 10, 2021, https://www.history.com/news/memorial-day-civil-war-slavery-charleston. Accessed June 28, 2021.

ing service to help the spirits of the lost ones travel well. Weeks before, the *New York Times* had published their own list of one thousand names on the front page of their Sunday edition, volunteers for #NamingTheLost scoured the obituary pages of local newspapers for lives to honor and stories to tell. It was a soulful act of recovery and resurrection. A reminder that, at the end of the day, when institutions fail and norms collapse, we are in the words of Chance the Rapper, "All we got."[14]

By the time you read this, many more thousands will be added to the list, and some other tragedy possibly has captured the world's attention. What I do know is that, in this tragedy and those yet to come, the victims deserve to have their names spoken. They each deserve to know that their life mattered to someone somewhere. So, we speak their names as a spiritual practice of collective lament. We feel the bone-deep sorrow of our neighbors and help them carry it, lest they become subsumed and believe the pernicious lie that they are alone. We don sackcloth and ashes. We moan. We weep. We sit shiva. We dance. We pour libations. We sing. We light candles. We chant.

... Elvu Davis, Elvester McKoy, Elworth Anthony Gibson, Elwyte Gardner, Emilio S. Allué, Emmy Falta, Enekee Leake-Cherry, Eric Murray, Ernestine Miles Mann, Ernesto Guzman, Esequiel "Zeke" Cisneros, Esperanza Tapia de Mayorga, Estelita Solomon, Ethel Wright, Eugene Thompson, Eulalio Rodriguez, Eva Candelaria, Evelyn Alda Seckler, Ezequiel Ortiz, Francis "Mike" Hugo, Fadel Erian, Faralyn Havir, Father Gioacchino Basile, Father Hilary Rodgers, Father Jorge Ortiz-Garay, Felicia Ailende, Feliks Ogorodnik, Felix Jimenez, Florastine Young, Floyd Bluntson, Frances Jansen, Frances Williamson, Francis "Frankie" Molinari, Francis "Frank" Boccabel-

[14] Chance the Rapper, "All We Got," track 1 on *Coloring Book*, 2016, Accessed July 2, 2021. https://open.spotify.com/album/71QyofYesSsRMwFOTafnhB?highlight=spotify:track:3ZLyt2ndLFBh148XRYjYYZ

la III, Frank A.M. Williams, Frank Keating, Frank Massey, Frank Miszkiewicz, Franklin D. Williams Jr., Franklin Williams, Fred Gallo, Fred Harris, Fred Simon, Fred Stauffer, Frederick "Fritz" Koerner, Frederick Carl Harris, Frederick Sands, Frederick Schwab, Gabriel de Jesus Marin Serna, Garry Bowie, Garry Bowie, Gary Holmberg, Gary J. Baptist, Gary Povar, Gary Walker, Gene Wilkinson, George Culetsu, George Henry Croom Jr., George J. Foerst Jr., George Matthews Jr., George McKibben, George Parrott Jr., George Possas, George Siegel, George Valentine, George Zeh, Gerald Edwards, Gerald Glenn, Gerald Slater, Gerald Welch, Gerard Bartuch, Gertrude Jones, Gil Torres, Gilbert Constant, Gilbert Joseph Strain III, Gilbert L. Barnes Sr., Giuseppi (Joseph) Logan, Glenda Hopkins ...

We remember. We remember. We remember that ...

We heal. I believe that our healing begins when we allow our sadness to wash over us like a baptismal font, cleansing us of our apathy, helping us recall our precarious mortality. We are vulnerable, yes, but we also are connected. Isolated, but interdependent. Lonely, but not alone.

> *You turned my wailing into dancing;*
> *you removed my sackcloth and clothed me with joy,*
> *that my heart may sing your praises and not be silent*
> *Lord my God, I will praise you forever.*

Psalm 30:11-12 (NIV)

May your memory continue to be a comfort to all those who mourn you.

Love,
A Woman Wailing for the Lost

Imagination: What Wants to Emerge?

"It started that way: laughing children, dancing men, crying women and then it got mixed up. Women stopped crying and danced; men sat down and cried; children danced, women laughed, children cried until, exhausted and riven, all and each lay about the Clearing damp and gasping for breath. In the silence that followed, Baby Suggs, holy, offered up to them her great big heart.

She did not tell them to clean up their lives or go and sin no more. She did not tell them they were the blessed of the earth, its inheriting meek or its glorybound pure.

She told them that the only grace they could have was the grace they could imagine. That if they could not see it, they would not have it."

— Toni Morrison, *Beloved*

Composting Religion

A Letter to Spiritual Leaders on the Edge[15]

Dear Beloved,

I come from a family of Black women who conjure life out of the soil. More than gardeners, they are divine stewards of the earth. Watching my mama tend to her plants was one of my favorite pastimes growing up. Each year, she took time to carefully select the variety of flowers she would plant, taking stock of what was in season and what was preparing to bloom. I never had a green thumb myself, but I always marveled at the way she coaxed something beautiful from a patch of dirt.

During her more ambitious years, she attempted to keep a vegetable patch, but always with limited success. The tomato plants never quite yielded the fruit she hoped. The cucumbers were always puny. The soil in our backyard, she complained, was just not right for the seeds.

I think it stung her a bit because her mother, Harriet, always had gorgeous, expansive vegetable gardens that seemed in my young eyes to go on infinitely. There were pole beans, turnip and mustard greens, and occasionally peppers. When we visited each

---

[15] This letter was adapted from a speech entitled "Composting" written and delivered by Jennifer Bailey at TedxSkoll at Oxford University on April 7, 2017. As of July 17, 2021, the full address can be found online at https://www.youtube.com/watch?v=eAkqO75a1js

summer, we always returned home with a cooler packed full of its bounty to sustain us for the winter.

My granny was born in an agricultural community on the cusp of Florida's Panhandle and raised in the fields of southern Georgia during the Great Depression. The failure of the Reconstruction project in the South gave rise to new forms of oppressive agricultural practices—tenant farming, sharecropping, and wage labor—that indebted Black laborers to white landowners. Lynching and other forms of racial terrorism, paired with Jim and Jane Crow laws, became tools of enforcement that guaranteed continued domination by white people in the social hierarchy.

While FDR's New Deal promised relief to some segments of the American population, key components of the new social contract, including the Social Security Act of 1935, intentionally excluded agricultural and domestic workers—industries dominated by Blacks. My grandmother and her family relied on the land to provide their sustenance and income. They kept livestock, grew their own food, and did what they needed to survive.

In the spring of 1941, as German bombs rained down over Liverpool and London, my nine-year-old grandmother was living with a different kind of terror. On the morning of May 15, 1941, the body of A.C. Williams, a young Black man in Quincy, Florida, was found lynched along the Withlacoochee River, five miles north of the city. His body, castrated and riddled with bullets, reduced his life to a public spectacle designed to psychically beat Quincy's Black community into submission to white supremacy.

For many families, migration became the only clear avenue for those seeking a better life for their loved ones. It was at the confluence of the Mississippi and Ohio Rivers that my grandmother disembarked from a Greyhound bus in Cairo, Illinois, in the early 1950s. Looking out over those two rivers, she felt what, until that moment, had been elusive in her life: hope.

On the soles of her shoes were traces of the earth from the small Southern town she'd left behind. She was eager to embark upon a new life, but she did not let go of the wisdom the land she'd left behind had taught her throughout her childhood. That knowledge would form the bedrock upon which her garden would sit and nourish her children and grandchildren for decades to follow. To this day, she is the least wasteful person that I know. Scraps of leftover fabric become quilting squares. Leftover food fertilizes the plants that later become the food on her table. My granny was *composting* before it became trendy.

* * *

In agriculture, the term *compost* is used to describe the recycling of organic waste materials through decomposition into a nutrient-rich organic fertilizer that improves soil fertility and biodiversity and prevents soil erosion. Simply put, using organic materials that are dying helps nurture the conditions that allow new life to grow. I have held this process close as I think about my own theological commitments as a clergyperson living in a time of religious transformation.

It is unsurprising to me that Black women would take up the metaphor of the garden as the core metaphor in the birth of womanism. Womanist theology is a form of reflection that places at its center the everyday experiences, moral perspectives, and religious worldview of Black women. In her 1983 book, *In Search of Our Mothers' Gardens*, Alice Walker provides a four-part definition of womanism. In it, Walker describes a womanist as a Black feminist who is, among other things, audacious and committed to the survival or all people. A womanist, Walker notes, "Loves music. Loves dance. Loves the moon. Loves the Spirit. Loves love and food and roundness. Loves struggle. Loves the Folk. Loves herself. Regardless."[16] In other words, to be a womanist is to embody a vision of radical hope that is grounded in the present.

The women in my family did not identify as *womanists*. They likely never heard the term before I came home from seminary with my hands filled with books and my head full of new ideas and a new vocabulary to talk about the way I experienced God. Even so, I could hear their voices between the lines of the texts I read. In the words of womanist theologians and ethicists like Katie Canon, M. Shawn Copeland, Delores Williams, Stacey Floyd-Thomas, and Emilie Townes, my beloved dean during my time at Vanderbilt Divinity School, I found a home that evoked the same feelings of belonging I had watching my mama and granny plant. Womanism felt like an invitation to me to reimagine a world grounded in an ever-expanding definition of love.

"Womanist theology," writes Townes, "takes old (traditional) religious language and symbols and gives them new (more diverse and complex) meaning."[17] It is composting work. The methodologies, writings, and transformational practices of womanism have become my gardening tools as I survey the landscape of American religious life today.

At first glance, the land appears barren. I am a millennial, and much has been written over the last decade about my generation's tendency to shy away from institutionalized forms of religious expression. Indeed, millennials and our Generation Z successors to the throne of youth are turning away from institutional religion faster than any other age group, raising a palpable sense of panic in religious communities concerned about their future.

---

[16] Alice Walker, *In Search of Our Mothers' Gardens: Womanist Prose* (San Diego: Harcourt Brace Jovanovich, 1984), xii.

[17] Emilie Townes, "Womanist Theology," https://ir.vanderbilt.edu/bitstream/handle/1803/8226/Townes-WomanistTheology.pdf?isAllowed=y&sequence=1

But I come from the Prairie State.

The American Midwest is famous for its endlessly flat topography. Driving through my home region can feel like a cruel and unusual form of punishment. On occasion, hours of corn, wheat, and soybean fields are broken up by a herd of cows or a winding river, only to return to the same monotony as before. It can be easy not to appreciate the bucolic beauty of the prairielands before you. To focus on what is immediately before your eyes, though, betrays the complex ecosystem of organisms, insects, and creatures at work beneath the surface. Even in the winter months, when the bounty of the fields gives way to empty plots, there is always something that wants to emerge.

The image of a barren field on the precipice of emergence feels like the *perfect* metaphor for the state of religious practice in the United States. When I fix my eyes on the horizon, I see rows of fruit and veggies in the form of new spiritually grounded communities and ritual practices waiting to sprout. They may not be recognizable to a casual observer searching for a congregation that meets on a weekly basis. For those seeking new forms of community to share in their questions and make meaning of their lives, these new varieties and hybrids may be the source of nourishment they have been longing for.

* * *

To understand the resistance of some members of my generation to traditional religious institutions is to understand our context. We grew up in the era in which pundits replaced professors and priests as the arbiters of facts. Our social and political identities were shaped against ongoing narratives of war and religious conflict. Information once available only in great libraries of storied academic institutions, we now carry in our pockets. Voices and experiences from around the world are just a click away. Amid the crowded landscape of new ideas, the loudest religious voices are those from the most polarized extremes—from pundits declaring any affront to "traditional values" a full out assault on Christianity to New Atheists boldly claiming that religion poisons everything. Even the nonreligious financial institutions that we were told to put our faith in because they were "too big to fail" faltered.[18]

Data from both Pew Research and the Public Religion Research Institute indicate that millennials and Gen Z are more socially tolerant of difference—particularly as it relates to race, gender expression and identity, and sexual orientation—than previous generations. For some young people, religion can be viewed as "too conservative" and "too intolerant" to make space for their values. Some scholars have asserted that this distinction in core values, alongside feelings of hurt or harm experienced from religion and religiously centered movements, are two factors contributing to the trend of young people disaffiliating from religious institutions as well as the growing number who identify as "spiritual, not religious," or with no religion at all.

Today we, as a global community, find ourselves warring over the vision of what we will become. At stake are the very souls of our communities, with battles being fought over kitchen tables, anonymous Internet comment sections, and at political rallies.

As racial and religious demographics continue to shift in many Western societies, it has brought along with it the potential for positive transformation *and* a well of anxiety and fear. It is this fear of change and difference, coupled with the instability of our economy, that has caused some among us to retreat into tribalism, clinging closely to those with whom they have much

---

[18] Jennifer Bailey, "Composting Religion," *The Huffington Post*, April 14, 2017, Composting Religion | HuffPost. https://www.huffpost.com/entry/composting-religion_b_58f0ee45e4b0156697224eab.

in common. We read and watch media sources that support only our opinions and biases. We live in communities with people like us. We demonize those who do not share our opinions. At its worst, this trend inflames our deeply held prejudices and leads to a violent scapegoating of those we brand "other," thus disregarding their humanity.

Against this backdrop, my friends and I have found a deep sense of moral meaning on the frontlines of movements—from climate justice to LGBTQ equality, universal healthcare to the creation of new economies. We've started businesses that value social impact as much as a financial bottom line. We've developed technologies that democratize access to knowledge. We've centered intersectionality as a core analysis for understanding how power works to maintain systems of inequality. Many of the core values traditionally ascribed to religious communities remain, even as the structures that cultivated them transform. Many of my peers are discovering new ways to express their deepest moral and ethical convictions, find community, and live into our "faith"—in humanity, in transformation, and yes, for some, in God.

There are several faith-affiliated groups making inroads on pressing social issues, from criminal justice reform to childhood poverty, by leveraging the power of community organizing networks such as Faith in Action, the Poor People's Campaign, Industrial Areas Foundation, and Faith in Public Life, to name a few. By and large, the role of religious identity and experience has been decentralized from contemporary social justice movements, even as young Gen Z and millennial organizers have sought to reintegrate spiritual practices and "collective care" spaces back into movement.

Even as movements for social justice have distanced themselves from institutionalized forms of religion, the *people* within those movements have increasingly expressed concern about a lack of sustainability, sustenance, and spiritual care in their movement spaces. Concerns that one might view as traditionally having been the domain of religious traditions.

Several years ago, my friend Carinne and I began a project called Rooted in Resilience, aimed at mapping the growing ecosystem of work being done to integrate personal and collective transformation, spiritual practice, and healing within frameworks for social change. Over the course of a year, we interviewed over seventy practitioners around the United States who were exploring the intersection of spirituality and social change. In our research and reporting we discovered the following:

> The emerging ecology of social movements today is a rejection of this highly professionalized, elite-facing organizing culture that arose in the '90s and into the Obama years, and simultaneously a constructive response to the ways in which movements have themselves been spaces of harm, recreating generation-old traumas and lines of division. Movements too often are sites of oppression and erasure where resource-scarcity favors individuals over the group, competition over collaboration, and where mistakes are turned into sources of shame and derision, instead of collectively-held lessons for future efforts. Some of the work at this intersection of social justice and spiritual/healing practice is a direct response to the inequity, fracture, and pain felt from within this subculture. For organizations to function like healthy organisms, and movements like thriving ecosystems, this must

be addressed and is. But birthing new norms, expectations, and practices takes structural investment and support.[19]

There is increasing demand for ways of being and grounding practices that center the full humanity of practitioners—body, mind, and soul. This desire stretches beyond frameworks of "self-care" to a more radically imagined "communal" or "squad" care model that centers the holistic well-being of both the individual and community. It feels deeply *womanist* to me. In response to this need, a proliferation of new programs, practices, and initiatives have taken shape.

These leaders are composting religion. They take the best of their lineages—the spiritual gardens of their foremothers—to fertilize the seedlings under their care while discarding that which no longer offers nutritional value. They are spiritual leaders who are interested in getting the training they need to meet this moment and serve with integrity—combining their need to "do something" and using the tools of their tradition to do it. Emerging vocational roles, like that of the movement chaplain, are in the process of defining themselves on how best to equip leaders with the knowledge and experience (if not "expertise") to serve in care-providing roles with integrity.

* * *

I am writing this letter to you, my fellow spiritual misfit, so that you know in no uncertain terms that you are not alone in your

[19] Rev. Jennifer Bailey and Carinne Luck, "Rooted in Resilience: Mapping the Expanding Horizons Where Social Justice, Spiritual Practice, and Healing Meet," (Faith Matters Network, 2020), https://static1.squarespace.com/static/53f25c8fe4b0014b3798ea58/t/5c1946810e2e720b4db9e4a7/1545160323699/Rooted+in+Resilience+-+Mapping+the+Horizons+of+Social+Justice+Spirituality+and+Healing.pdf.

quest for understanding your place in the world as it is evolving. At times it may feel like the earth is literally moving under your feet as you attempt to step in one direction or the other. That's because it is. All around us things are shifting, systems are collapsing, and institutions are failing. This should not surprise us. Around the world, elders across cultures and peoples were predicting this time would come. It is a time of great uncovering in which Mother Earth and Father Sky are pushing us into a divine reckoning about what it means to be in right relationship with one another and all sentient beings in the twenty-first century and beyond. It is clear to me that the actions we take now will have deep and irreversible consequences for the generations to come.

The good news is that this time is made for misfits.

When you are at the center of a circle, it is impossible to see what is at the perimeter—*if you are even aware that there is a perimeter*. As misfits who were pushed to the edges and in-between places, we are able to see what is on the horizon and collectively discern what is needed to meet the challenges ahead. We are called to be the gardeners who will compost and tend to the soil upon which future generations will sow seeds that will one day blossom. The little girl in me delights that my hours spent observing my mother plant were not in vain.

Those of us who are embedded within spiritual communities understand that there are roles within our religious communities that no longer serve us and fail to speak to the material conditions that shape the lives of our people. We cannot program our way out of crisis. No single curriculum will reverse the impact of climate change, end poverty, and heal more than four centuries of racial injustice in the United States. For far too long, we believed the insidious lie that innovation is the domain of those with the power and social status to determine what models are worthy of our attention and praise.

The enormity of the plight we face can be solved only by harnessing the ingenuity and creativity of the communities to which we belong and are accountable. This season will require us to *recover* ancestral wisdom and practices that we lost or undervalued, *repair* the deep breaches in our interpersonal and communal relationships that replicate patterns of harm and destruction, and *reimagine* the possible by stretching ourselves to see beyond the realities of our current circumstances and daring to dream something different into being.

These three words—*recover, repair,* and *reimagine*—remain at the center of my discernment process as I try to understand the evolution of my calling. My path is not linear. There are times I feel like I am chasing the shadow of something I cannot fully see. When I'm feeling particularly churchy, I wonder if that shadow is the Spirit of Divine Revelation. We can chase it, yearn for it, interpret it, but never *really* know its true form.

The great news is we do not have to take on these challenges alone. In the words of the great prayer created in honor of Bishop Oscar Romero, "We cannot do everything, and there is a sense of liberation in realizing that. This enables us to do something, and to do it very well." [20]

A model I have found helpful in thinking about these roles is one developed by South Asian American writer, strategist, lawyer, and racial justice advocate Deepa Iyer, who identifies ten roles within the social movement ecosystem, described below[21]:

- **Weavers:** See the through-lines of connectivity between people, places, organizations, ideas, and movements

---

[20] Ken Untener, "Prophets of a Future Not Our," https://www.usccb.org/prayer-and-worship/prayers-and-devotions/prayers/prophets-of-a-future-not-our-own.

[21] Building Movement Project, "Roles," https://buildingmovement.org/wp-content/uploads/2020/06/The-Roles-CC-BY-NC-SA-4.0.pdf

- **Experimenters:** Innovate, pioneer, and invent. I take risks and course-correct as needed

- **Frontline Responders:** Address community crises by marshaling and organizing resources, networks, and messages

- **Visionaries:** Imagine and generate our boldest possibilities, hopes and dreams, and remind us of our direction

- **Builders:** Develop, organize, and implement ideas, practices, people, and resources in service of a collective vision

- **Caregivers:** Nurture and nourish the people around me by creating and sustaining a community of care, joy, and connection

- **Disruptors:** Take uncomfortable and risky actions to shake up the status quo, to raise awareness, and to build power

- **Healers:** Recognize and tend to the generational and current traumas caused by oppressive systems, institutions, policies, and practices

- **Storytellers:** Craft and share our community stories, cultures, experiences, histories, and possibilities through art, music, media, and movement

- **Guides:** Teach, counsel, and advise, using my gifts of well-earned discernment and wisdom

As Iyer notes, "Not all of us can (or should) play each of these roles; an effective movement ecosystem requires different actors to play these roles. We might also find ourselves falling into different roles depending on personal and external circumstances."[22] As we can see from the map below, each of these

[22] Deepta Iyer, "Saying Goodbye to 2019's Seesaw of Outrage and Numbness," *Medium*, December 30, 2018, https://dviyer.medium.com/saying-goodbye-to-2018s-seesaw-of-outrage-and-numbness-5671aa6768df.

roles complement one another and build toward a collective vision of equity, liberation, justice, and solidarity for all.

What's My Role, Today?

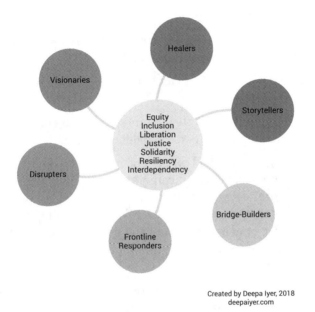

Created by Deepa Iyer, 2018
deepaiyer.com

As you take time to consider the unique role you are being called to fill in this season, I am reminded of a set of questions asked by one of our interviewees for the Rooted in Resilience project. She is a seasoned, self-identified Chicana and Latinx organizer in the Southwest who runs a network of thought leaders, historians, spiritual sages, trauma informed healers, and traditional and Western medicine practitioners working to center the wellbeing of and healing Latinx migrant peoples on the frontlines of the fight for migrant rights.

In evaluating these new roles and programs, she often asks:

1. Who are your teachers?
2. What is your practice?
3. What are the results of your practice?

Translated a different way:

1. From whom did you learn and how does that person understand where and how authority is granted?
2. Where do your practices come from and how do you embody them in your work?
3. How can your community guarantee that you are a reliable, trustworthy, and safe person to depend on?

Historically, we have relied on our authority being granted via ordination committees, certificate programs, or degrees from institutions of theological education. However, what I find most interesting is that many of the new roles and training programs we are initiating are being defined and developed *outside of these traditional spaces,* in some ways making these core questions all the more vital.

I hope that you find these frameworks and questions helpful as you begin to till the land. When the times get tough, I invite you to take a deep breath. You may never see the fruits of your labor, and that is in part the point. You are fertilizer, not seed. Cultivators, not harvesters. You are the continuation of a story of transformation, not the end.

Love,

An Amateur Gardener Tending to the Soil

Looking Back, Moving Forward:
Letter to a Young Griot

Dear Beloved,

I am writing to you because you are the keeper of stories that will pass down to the generations yet to be born. From time immemorial, your forebearers in Mali, Senegal, and other parts of West Africa have served as living repositories of oral traditions and handed down family and community history from one generation to the next. You are troubadour-historians. The progenitors of your lineage played the balafon and kora to sing the story of their ancestors. Some still do to this day. My Beloved Young Griot, you are creating new instruments and technologies to shape the narratives that will carry and sustain us as we move into the future. Your work has never been more important.

I am writing to you from the year 2021. A new world is yearning to emerge. All around there is a deepening sense of reckoning afoot as the tides of change crash into walls of resistance. These are tense and turbulent times. In the United States, we have political leaders playing footsie with fascism. Their acolytes, drunk on a constant stream of misinformation and bigotry, are willing to die rather than live in a multiracial democracy in which they have to share power. Still others in their camp live in a reality defined by grievance. They believe themselves the victim of a coordinated attack against the America they once knew. They have bought into the myth of scarcity and cannot fathom a context in which there is enough for all to flourish.

Even so, my faith dooms me to be an optimist. That optimism is not born out of naivete, rather it is the product of a commitment to practice hope each day. As a Black girl in America, I learned a long time ago that to keep living is itself an act of willful defiance against the death-dealing forces of hate that would see me and my kindred eradicated and erased from the tomes of history.

It is my intuition that if we are to ride the waves of uncertainty toward the promise of a transformed world, we must speak and live the truth of where we have been and where we are going. Yet even the concept of truth is contested in this season, which is why I am calling on you.

When you tell the story of these times, with their fresh round of protests against systemic violence, do not forget that behind each great movement for justice are tales of everyday indignities faced by folks who fought to snatch their humanity back from those who would seek to steal it from them. More often than not, it is these experiences that move people to act.

That was certainly the case for me. The first time I was made to feel less than human because of the color of my skin was on the playground at Adams Elementary School. I was five years old.

The year was 1992, and across the United States the air was thick with racial tension. In April of that year, the City of Los Angeles caught on fire. A videotape of Los Angeles police brutally beating an unarmed Black man named Rodney King had sparked a long simmering fuse of resentment about the treatment of communities of color by those sworn to protect and serve them. When the officers were acquitted, a bomb of bitterness exploded, giving life to the immortal words of the Rev. Dr. Martin Luther King, "A riot is the language of the unheard."

This was not the first time LA had burned. On August 11, 1965, a California Highway Patrol officer pulled over a twenty-one-year old African American man named Marquette Frye for reckless driving. Frye and his brother Ronald were driving home from an afternoon drinking and celebrating with two female acquaintances. As officers gave Marquette a field sobriety test, Ronald walked home to alert their mother, Rena. What transpired after Rena arrived on the scene is disputed.[23] What *is* known is that the encounter escalated, and rumors quickly began to spread throughout the family's Watts neighborhood that the LAPD had beaten Rena and a pregnant bystander. According to reports, that night over 1,500 people took to the streets.[24]

Let me pause here. When I first learned about this history, I must admit I was surprised that at the center of this animating event was a community responding to acts of violence against Black women. In our contemporary racial justice movements, so much of our attention is drawn to acts of brutality inflicted upon cisgender Black men. We know the names of Emmett Till, Rodney King, Trayvon Martin, Mike Brown, and George Floyd, as we should. Yet with the notable exception of Sandra Bland and Breonna Taylor, we find it hard to #sayhername.

For six days, Watts stirred as thousands of residents emerged to air their deeply held grievances.

Buildings looted. Cars destroyed. Stores set ablaze. In an all too familiar refrain, the echoes of which can be heard in our current discourse, some would characterize the events of those days as a crazed mob frenzy; others an uprising. I would simply describe it as Black pain on public display that refuses to be silenced. Anxiety and panic quickly spread among white residents of the

---

[23] Gerald Horne, *Fire This Time: The Watts Uprising and the 1960s* (Charlottesville, VA: University of Virginia Press, 1995), 54.

[24] Horne, 57.

city. Fear that the angry images of Black men and women they saw on their television sets would soon arrive at their doorstep. On August 13, Governor Pat Brown succumbed to pressure and called in the California National Guard to aid local police in extinguishing the rebellion. When the embers finally calmed, thirty-four people were dead and more than $40 million in property damage reported.

Twenty-seven years later, Americans watched frozen in horror as, once again, Los Angeles erupted. The lingering smell of soot from burnt out buildings in Los Angeles permeated the atmosphere and stretched across the country to small towns like the one I called home. I spent my childhood in a quintessential Midwestern town far from the bright lights of Hollywood. It is the kind of place where residents are content with staying in the ways of the past, yet reluctantly being pushed forward by the reality of time. The Mississippi River is its life source, giving birth to the industry and commerce that sustains the 40,000 people who call it home. Pickup trucks often outnumber cars in grocery store parking lots. The county fair and Knights of Columbus barbecue are the highlights of the summer calendar. Season tickets to the high school basketball games are a hot commodity. When political pundits speak of the "real America" nestled just beyond the cornfields where God and country still matter, they are referring to places like the one where I grew up.

America's Heartland is not without its shadows. Scratch just beneath the veneer of nostalgia and you will find a more complicated set of truths. Just past the well-manicured lawns are doors that lead to hushed stories that are rarely uttered aloud. There is the former Marine finally home from two tours of duty in the Middle East. He cannot find employment because his memory will not allow him to escape the horrors that he has seen. There is the soccer mom whose addiction to prescription pain pills has led her to seek more potent highs. There are the children going to bed hungry for another night because the factory where their parents worked downsized and they have not been able to find steady work since. Applying for food stamps is a humiliation they cannot bear. Theirs are stories of resentment, misplaced hopes, and shattered dreams. It is no wonder that yearning for the "good old days" has become a regular lament. When the right messenger came at the opportune time, promising to "Make America Great Again," the message was met with a fervent enthusiasm usually reserved for tent revivals or trips to the state championship.

To be clear, when folks in my hometown speak about what made America great, their vision is decidedly monochromatic. Those who call themselves white make up nearly 90 percent of the population, with many tracing their ancestral lineage back to the same collection of villages in Germany. It is the kind of place where unity has come to mean sameness. Thus, those who fall outside the realm of that which is considered normal are pushed to the fringes. Those branded "other" often find themselves confined to the "North Side" of town, a community where poor white and Black folk are united in their experiences of Jesus and jails, limited opportunities, and lowered expectations.

From the beginning, we were outsiders. My parents failed to check the neat boxes that presumed their race and class identity defined them as poor and Black. They were explorers in uncharted territory. College-educated city folk who moved to the country. I was two years old when my parents loaded our car and left our loved ones on the Southside of Chicago to move West, where short-term résumé booster jobs would propel the careers of these college-educated city folk.

I have very few memories of this time, but one that remains prominent is one of my mother's tear-filled eyes dropping me off at day care for the first time. I can still see the fluorescently lit hallway in the basement of the hospital where she worked as she handed me over into the beige-toned arms of a woman whose name escapes me now. Mama had been reared by her extended family in a Black community that celebrated its proud heritage and told its dark-hued children they were precious. This was not that place. Its stark white walls and bulletin boards were full of playful images of white children existing happily in an all-white world that had no room for her kinky-haired child. As she turned to walk away, I can only imagine the terrified uncertainty she must have felt as she turned her back to move toward the door. What I know for sure is that between my tears I started to scream.

I began kindergarten three years later with bright eyes excited to finally join the big kids in the enterprise of learning. My day care experience had not been the nightmare of my mother's worst dreams. In fact, I thrived as precocious toddlers with loving parents often do. I even had a squad. Katie, Renee, and I saw ourselves as incarnations of characters from our favorite television show *The Rugrats*. I was Tommy Pickles, a troublemaker on a tricycle always in search of an adventure.

Next on my list of feats to conquer was this thing called school. I was preparing for this moment my whole life. Daddy was an educator. He worked with grown-ups who dropped out of school when they were young, only to return later in life to earn the equivalent of their high school diploma. About 10 percent of the people in our community lacked basic literacy skills. One of my dad's many jobs was teaching them how to read. I would often accompany him to his classes. He would set me up in the back of the room with a book on tape and coloring books while he explained the basics of phonics to elders who had left their formal schooling to work on family farms when they were not that much older than me.

Sometimes I would take off my headphones and just listen, sounding out and spelling words along with the rest of the class. I loved it. I loved the way that the letters rolled off my tongue. I loved the puzzle of figuring out which sounds matched the images on the chalkboard and on the papers in front of me. By the time I reached my fourth birthday, I knew how to read. Daddy promised me that in this magical place called kindergarten I would learn to read longer books and so much more. So I packed my best Little Mermaid backpack and made my way, holding each of my parent's hands and smiling about the possibilities.

That first day, the boundaries of my world grew. Adams Elementary School was unlike any place I had known. It was gigantic. The hallways seemed endless. There were computer labs and a big gym with basketball hoops. There was a library stacked full of books that seemed to extend above my head just like my dad said. By far, the biggest shock was the playground. It was four times as big as the one at my day care center. There were multiple slides and monkey bars. It was a wonderland full of potential for countless adventures beyond my wildest dreams.

As excited as I was about the physical landscape, I soon learned that navigating the social landscape of recess was an incredibly difficult process.

One day, behind the tire swings, a boy named Evan approached me at recess, confidently stating that I must be dirty and rotten because why else would my skin be brown? As the other children laughed profusely, I became acutely aware of my status as the "other." My skin was indeed brown and as much as I tried to wash it off, I soon realized there was nothing I could do to change it. One day, at the apex of the bullying, I was called a "nigger" for the first time. Thus began my education into the complex history of race relations in the United States.

Throughout the year, the taunts and comments would escalate with little intervention from teaching staff that had never been trained on how to engage difference. I was the only child of color in my classroom. Living in the shadow of Rodney King and a re-invigorated national conversation on race relations, the impulse among many white people in my community was to ignore the presence of racism. To acknowledge it, they surmised, would only lead to discord and discomfort.

Somewhere along the way in the post-Civil Rights era, a racist became the worst thing you could call a white person. If the images of Watts burning elicited fear among white communities, then videos of police officers attacking peaceful protestors in crisp business suits in Selma with dogs and water hoses stoked their shame. Shame is a hell of a drug. It paralyzes rather than propels. It keeps people stuck. Rather than embrace the Civil Rights era as an uncovering that could break open a real conversation about racial equity and speak truth about the damages of white supremacy, white America grew tired of being shown their shadows and assumed a defensive posture. It heard the clarion call of dog-whistle politics and discovered terms like "color blindness" and "reverse racism" to push back against demands for Black liberation.

In the schoolyard of my childhood, I learned from my white teachers the common reaction of "good" white people when confronted directly by the ugly realities of racism: they deflect. My teachers nodded their heads in sympathy, repeating platitudes meant to de-escalate the tension. On my more compassionate days, I can find an echo of empathy for them within my spirit. You do not prioritize that which you are not taught is important. They lived in an all-white world and my presence was a disruption they were not equipped and trained to handle. They failed to respond to my racial trauma for the same reasons they sent me home each year during the annual school head lice check, despite the fact never once did my mama find evidence of an infestation. The kinkiness of my hair, like the discrimination I lived through, was just too hard for them to understand and navigate.

But when I see photos of myself from this time, my rage burns anew. There is a noticeable weariness in my face that ages me far beyond my years. Black girls are so unprotected. Perhaps most insidiously, we are not deemed *worthy* of protection. People do not notice when the light behind our eyes begins to dim, nor are they observant enough to ask why.

First wounds can cut the deepest. For years I internalized the lie that I was inferior. Despite robust deprogramming efforts from my parents and community, it took decades of prayer and therapy for me to start believing that my early experiences of racial discrimination were not my fault. To this day I find myself, from time to time, working to counteract the unrelenting voices in my head that tell me I am not worthy. I would not wish the experience upon anyone.

I know that in order to move forward, I have to look back. Like the Sankofa bird, we are holding the future in our beaks while learning from the past in order to bring that knowledge into the present. Remembering is an act of resurrection. Only fools think that it is wise to start from scratch. Each time we recall what we have learned and choose to let that knowledge inform our actions, we build on the foundation laid by our ancestors.

Young Griot, as you travel from place to place, singing the hymns of our histories and reclaiming the traditions that those who seek our destruction would have us forget, don't you forget to ask your audience to add their stories to the canon. I have found that the act of rememory—putting back together the shards of broken memories and forgotten horrors—to be vital in my healing from racial trauma. Our stories are a shield against those who would seek to gaslight me and deny my experience. In sharing them, I am reminded that I am not alone. In our collective witness, I find the strength to keep pressing on.

Love,

A Fellow Wanderer Finding Her Way

You Are Beautiful. You Are Brave

A Love Letter to the Child in My Belly

Dear Beloved,

Your grandma taught me how to pray. As the day turned to evening and I donned the fuzzy footie pajamas that were a staple of my childhood, I would crawl into bed as she tucked me in, whispering words of love into my ear. *You are beautiful. You are brave. You are God's beloved one.*

What I did not know then was that these were ancient words. Words passed down from Black mothers to their children in slave quarters and cotton fields, shotgun houses and urban ghettos. Prophetic utterances that affirmed the humanity of Black children in a world that did not love them back. They are radical words shaped on the road between Sarah's longing and Hagar's cries for deliverance. They are visions of a future not yet come to pass: A world in which all babies can freely dream and hope and create and wonder and live without the threat of violence looming like a thief in the night.

As I prepare to welcome you into the world, I've been thinking a lot about The Mothers of the Movement. These women are a sisterhood of sorrow whose children were killed on the altar of white supremacy—by vigilantes, commissioned foot soldiers of the empire, and police officers who were trained not to see those women's babies as human, but rather part of a problem that only blood sacrifice could solve. I imagine Wanda Cooper-Jones sitting by her window waiting for her son, Ahmaud Arbery, to come home from his run. Tamika Palmer longing to hear her baby Breonna Taylor's voice one last time. If angels do indeed cry, I wonder if Mamie Till wiped the tears from Larcenia Jones Floyd's eyes as George cried out for her in his last moments. I hope that I am never initiated into this sorority of suffering, yet recognize with a degree of resignation that in accepting the call to Black motherhood, I cannot and must not avert my eyes from the spectacle of Black death before me.

In a spirit of solemnity, I will have to sit you down one day, my beautiful baby, and tell you that there are those in this world who will seek to kill you—not just your physical body, but your dreams. It may sound ridiculous, and I must confess that there is a part of me that feels absurd writing this, but in my limited time here on earth I have found that the latter is far more dangerous than the former. One death is after the destruction of your temporal body, the other is an act of soul murder that lingers. As the great Bard of Harlem, Langston Hughes, pondered many moons ago, a dream deferred has the potential to "dry up like a raisin in the sun," withering under the suffocating heat of naysayers and haters who do not have your best interest at heart. I promise to speak life into you against the beating drum of forces that would seek to do you harm. I will affirm you and love you with a full-throated chorus of affirmations loud enough to shake the foundations of the earth.

There also will be people who seek to define who you are. They will tell you that as a mixed-race child born of a Black woman and Jewish man, you will have to make specific choices about your identity. You, my sweet love, contain multitudes. The only choices that you *have* to make in this regard are the ones you decide to explore. As you set forth on the road to discovering who you are, I thought it might be helpful for you to know who your people are. Your lineage is a compass. If you let it, your lineage can be a helpful tool that helps guide you when you are feeling lost and locates you in a broader narrative of history.

You are the descendent of those who survived pogroms and concentration camps, chattel slavery and the terrorism of Jim and Jane Crow. Your genealogy is full of stories of death and determination, pain and perseverance, sorrow and salvation, tragedy and triumph. Your body is a monument to history. In your DNA are the hidden tales of those forgotten to the great epics of antiquity *and* a living chronicle that charts generations of geopolitical struggle. You come from people who worked the earth in shtetls and on tenet farms and coaxed from barren lands the fruits of harvest. You are a part of their harvest. You are the answer to prayers whispered softly into the darkness of night under the watchful gaze of unnamed stars that heard their yearnings and answered, *"Soon."*

From your father you inherit a place in the *kohanim*—the priestly cast that the Torah describes as dating back to the days of Aaron. It is a holy demarcation bound in a *covenant of salt* [25] and meant to last. On the High Holidays, when you come of age, you will ascend the bimah with your dad and grandfather and offer the ancient words of the Birkat Kohahim, the Priestly Blessing, over the congregation offering words of protection, favor, and peace to those gathered.

In my bloodline are Spirit-filled preachers and teachers who built shrines to the Divine in hush harbors and dusty backroads. They were practitioners of what Mama Ruby Sales calls Black folk religion:

---

[25] Numbers 18:19: "All the heave-offerings of the holy things, which the children of Israel offer unto the LORD, have I given thee, and thy sons and thy daughters with thee, as a due for ever; it is an everlasting covenant of salt before the LORD unto thee and to thy seed with thee.'" (JPS Tanakh 1917).

It was a religion that combined the ideals of American democracy with a theological sense of justice. It was a religion that said that people who were considered property and disposable were essential in the eyes of God and even essential in a democracy, although we were enslaved. And it was a religion where the language and the symbols were accessible, that the God talk was accessible to even 7-year-olds.[26]

It is their faith that forms the bedrock of my own. I imagine that it won't always be easy having a clergywoman as your mom. You likely will see the ugliness that can take root in the hearts of even the most sanctified people. Be patient with them when you can. Set boundaries and keep your distance when you must. Nothing is more important to me than protecting your peace.

So when anyone seeks to deny the sacredness of your life, you can declare with confidence that you know who you are. You come from hallowed stock. You are the apple of God's eye. But here's the secret that many fail to understand: So is every living thing. I believe the presence of the Divine can be found anywhere if you look hard enough, yet it is sometimes obscured by the wickedness and evil born of ideologies and theologies that seek domination over creation. Throughout your life you will be socialized into a culture that is built on the death-dealing lie of scarcity, that there is not enough—resources, money, food, shelter, and [fill in the blank], for everyone to thrive.

When my thoughts tarry too long in the valley of the shadow of death, I remember my mama's prayer. I am comforted by the words of a mentor who recently peered over the rim of her rainbow glasses, looked me in the eye, and reminded me that

---

[26] Krista Tippet, "Ruby Sales: Where Does It Hurt," On Being, podcast audio, September 15, 2016, https://onbeing.org/programs/ruby-sales-where-does-it-hurt.

having a baby in this moment in history is an act of radical hope. You are an expression of radical hope. A hope born out of the possibility of what can be rather than what it is. I feel blessed that the feeling of radical hope is never far from me. That in the words of an old hymn, "Morning by morning new mercies I see."[27] I see those mercies in the faces of young activists and elders leading us into a space of creativity and imagination by helping us dream about what "public safety" *could* be in the twenty-first century. I feel it in the way your dad gently rubs my belly at night, whispering his own words of adoration for you as you reward us with kicks and wiggles. I taste it in fresh peaches at my local farm stand.

As a Christian raised in the Black Church, my faith is rooted in the rituals and practices of Black mamas and church mothers whose wisdom and steadfast belief in God were passed to me through quiet conversations in church kitchens and choir rehearsal pews. They taught me that although time is filled with swift transition,[28] while change and uncertainty are the only things of which we can be certain, the God of our foremothers could and will sustain us. The air in our lungs is living proof.

You are living proof. Pregnancy is a period of preparation. I am finding that one of the many miracles of this time is discovering just how powerful my body and the bodies of all birthing parents are. For a limited time, you and I are sharing one body that holds two hearts, two spirits, and two life stories that are unfolding. Even now as you kick at my ribs and make space for yourself in our shared container, I am reminded of both the joy and precarity of life. Even before you enter the world, you are shaping it because you are already transforming the lives of those around you. In these turbulent and uncertain times, the very announcement

---

[27] "Great Is Thy Faithfulness," by Thomas Chisholm [PD].

[28] "Hold to God's Unchanging Hand," by Jennie Wilson [PD].

of your impending arrival is a light and respite for many thirsting to drink at the well of possibility and optimism. You have blessed them without uttering a word.

I truly believe those blessings have been deeply felt, in part, because of the context in which you are arriving. I did not intend to give birth to you in the midst of a global pandemic, but here we are. Today, the global community finds itself battling a common enemy in COVID-19 that is literally seeking to steal our breath. The words of George Floyd and Eric Garner and so many unknown and unnamed—"I Can't Breathe"—have become a rallying cry for racial justice. As the coronavirus pandemic continues to devastate our communities, I've found myself longing to hear my mama's sweet whisperings again. She died four years ago on Mother's Day eve and I miss her every day. While her body is gone, her spirit looms large, as do the lessons from grieving her loss.

This spring, before you were born, I heard an elder, Roshi Joan Halifax, share that grief is love that has nowhere to go. So many of us are grieving in this season, whether the loss of a loved one or the loss of a dream or expectation or opportunity. When we are at our best, we are able to see grief as a pathway to deeper love—a love that opens us up to see the deep humanity in one another, a deeper appreciation for the earth as our Mother, and deeper connection to all living things.

Finally, please know that I will get it wrong sometimes, too. One thing I want you to understand from the start of our time together is that your mama is not perfect. I have my own scars that sometimes guide me to make a less than courageous choice out of fear. The same tongue that will affirm and love you may, without question, one day hurt you. We will disagree. We will argue. We will say things to one another that we will wish we could take back. I want to begin the practice of apologizing to you when I have caused you harm early in your life, no matter how many months and years you have under your belt. You see, sometimes grown-ups have a hard time acknowledging the validity of children's feelings or assume the pain they cause will be forgotten or fade away. I know this is not the case. I have spent many hours in tears with therapists attempting to reckon with unaddressed trauma from my youth. I value your mental and spiritual well-being as much as your physical health. It is with a spirit of deep humility that I offer you this vow: To remember that we are on a mutual learning journey and you have as much to teach me as I have to teach you.

You are beautiful. You are brave. You are God's beloved one. I cannot wait to meet you.

Love,

Your Mama

Max Elisha was born on September 13th, 2020 full of magic, wonder, and light.

Living: What Is Already Blooming Beautifully in the World?

"Freeing yourself was one thing, claiming ownership of that freed self was another."

— Toni Morrison, *Beloved*

At the Table

A Letter to My Fellow Foodies in Search of A Communal Table[29]

Dear Beloved,

The only thing I know how to make from scratch is my granny's sweet potato pie. I learned to make it by peeking from behind her housecoat as she danced through each ritual of the pie-making process with grace and agility. The first pirouette glided us out to her backyard garden where her fingers met the dirt and pulled each potato from the earth, one by one. She then twirled between peeling, boiling, mashing, and sweetening the batter until it tasted just right. All the while she told me stories about our history. Most often she spoke about our ancestral homeland in southern Georgia. At the turn of the twentieth century, her grandfather purchased a tract of land amid the tall, skinny pines. This untamed wilderness became our family's homestead for nearly one hundred years. With sweat on their brow, the men and women whose blood runs through my veins prepared the ground for seed in a quest for a bountiful harvest.

---

[29] This letter is a revised from an article originally published by Jennifer Bailey on January 16, 2017 entitled, "I Am the Breathing Legacy of One of America's Great Original Sins" for The On Being Project. As of June 28, 2021, the original text can be found online at https://onbeing.org/blog/i-am-the-breathing-legacy-of-one-of-america-s-great-original-sins. Many thanks to the On Being team for the permission to reprint portions of the article here.

Here she learned to honor dirt as the site of new life and sustenance. Her stories then always turned to the little brick church her uncle built on the same track of land. It was a place, she said, where you could taste the Spirit of God as the noonday sun reflected onto the wall shadows of the plants that adorned the fields. When the stories concluded, we wrapped up the warm baked pie and carried it around the corner to her church. Once there, we placed it in the church kitchen among a feast of cakes, covered dishes, dinner rolls, chicken, and ham. As I gazed hungrily at the variety of dishes on the table, I wondered how many other little girls and boys peeked from behind their grandmother's housecoat and found their history.

My culinary knowledge is limited, but God knows that I can eat. Few things in life bring me more joy than discovering an amazing restaurant or trying a new type of cuisine. Highbrow or hole-in-the wall, I love it all. The first bite of a hot beef patty, feeling the steam of a fresh bowl of pho on my upper lip, the sound of my spoon cracking the caramelized shell of crème brûlée, that moment when the macaroni and cheese touches the candied yams on my Thanksgiving dinner plate—there is no question that some of my best memories are food related.

The past four years I have made a habit of having dinner with strangers. A few days after the 2016 presidential election, two friends and I created a project called People's Supper, which uses shared meals to build trust and connection among people of different identities and perspectives. To date, we have hosted more than 2,000 of these conversations in homes, public libraries, church basements, school cafeterias, and online Zoom rooms. At last count, 10,000 people have gathered around potluck dinner tables in over 100 cities and towns nationwide.

The People's Supper was born on a historic highway far from the coastal lands that tend to burn the brightest national spotlight. On November 15, 2016, I was driving from my home in Nashville, Tennessee, to a work commitment in Little Rock, Arkansas, when I called my friend Lennon to keep me company. The road from Nashville to Little Rock stretches approximately 350 miles through the winding hills of Middle Tennessee, across the Mississippi River, to the foot of the Ozark Mountains. It is America's heartland. The place where Midwest-nice meets Southern hospitality by creating a culture of warmth that sometimes obscures the chilling history of racial animus and economic exploitation lingering beneath the surface. Just off the interstate are small towns filled with people whom time has forgotten. Communities with sweet names like Cherry Valley and Sugar Tree waiting with bitter resolve for salvation that never came. Nearly 60 million Americans live in rural areas with sweet names and complex pasts that until recently have been an afterthought. Homesteads long departed. Memories locked away in fading family photo albums in suburban basements and big city condos. Roots severed.

Lennon and I talked about a lot that day. We talked about our fear and anxiety about the world that was to come. We reflected that we should have seen this coming. As technology has given us access to more information, it has had the unintended consequence of drawing us more deeply into our own echo chambers as we seek voices that think, act, and believe as we do. We watch cable news programs that confirm our biases. We dismiss news sources that do not fit our worldview as biased.

At its worst, this trend inflames our deeply held prejudices and leads to a violent scapegoating of those we brand "other," thus robbing them of their humanity. It is this logic of dominance that plays out in our media when the instinct is to brand Black men as criminals, immigrants as illegals, and Muslims as terrorists. For some of us whose identities are often placed at the margins of our society, the decline in our relationships with one another is not a complete surprise. As James Baldwin once said, "To be a Negro in this country and to be relatively conscious is to be in a rage almost all the time."[30] It is a rage born out of a sense of righteous indignation. We know that institutions built to privilege some and exploit others are fundamentally violent because it has been our experience throughout the history of this nation. Justice has never been given freely to us and has always required blood sacrifices from those bold enough to demand it.

More than anything else, Lennon and I talked about grief. I had lost my mom six months prior. Lennon's mom died when she was in college. Several years before the conversation we had during my road trip, she co-founded an organization called The Dinner Party, a platform for grieving twenty- and thirty-some-things to find peer community and build lasting relationships. What started as a group of friends sharing openly about their experiences of loss after the death of a loved one became a movement to transform some of our hardest conversations and most isolating experiences into sources of community support, candid conversation, and forward movement using the age-old practices of gathering and breaking bread. It was clear to us both that our country was in mourning and had been for a long time. So we wondered aloud what it would look like to apply some of the lessons about death learned from The Dinner Party to a broader civic context. We called our friend Emily, a movement building genius, and two months later the first People's Suppers began.

We understood that for millennia, sharing a meal has stood as one of the few things that all of us—whoever we are and wherever we come from—have in common. Sitting at a common

---

[30] *Time* magazine, August 1965.

table to break bread is one of humanity's most ancient and simple rituals. Tables are places where we can share meaningful stories, good food, and a sense of community. A place where we can build the relationships and trust upon which the work of community building depends.

Sharing a meal is a deeply theological commitment for me. I believe that God is hungry and waiting to be fed. You can see God's hunger in the eyes of seniors choosing between purchasing medication and buying groceries for the week. You can hear God's hunger pains in the pews of my grandmother's church, uttered from the grumbling bellies of children whose only meal of the day will be the one they receive after service. The notion of the hungry God has deep roots in African American theological thought. A defining characteristic of Black theology is a strong emphasis on the immanence of God in the daily lives of Black folk.

When Christians partake in the sacrament of holy communion, the body of the Christ is handed over to us as we feed one another. This body is the mythical body of the Lord incarnate. Thus, when we eat of his flesh and drink of his blood, we nourish ourselves and are emboldened with the triumphant power of the resurrection to disrupt the status quo, overcome systemic racism, and challenge white supremacy. This resurrection power is the same energy that Paul speaks of in Ephesians 3:20, "Now to him who by the power at work within us is able to accomplish abundantly far more than all we can ask or imagine." In the communion moment we are enfleshed with the power of Christ to combat inequity in the world, an experience that womanist theologian M. Shawn Copeland calls "eucharistic solidarity." Eucharistic solidarity is then the act of both re-membering *and* embodying the love of Christ. In Christ's body we recognize both the horrific terror oppression reaps on bodies and the hope of the resurrection embodied through action to overcome that oppression.

I have spent time sitting across tables from people whose life stories were wildly different from mine. There was the Chicana elder who labored with her family of migrant farm workers under the harsh conditions of California's fruit orchards for wages that often were withheld or outright stolen. There was the conservative pastor from rural North Carolina who shared openly about his father's alcoholism and abuse. There was the college senior, a refugee from Somalia, who could not fathom the entitlement and ingratitude of his peers who complained about the options in the dining halls. Each story was sacred. Each personal account taught me a little bit more about the rich strands of experience that make up the American narrative.

I am grateful for the time I invested at those tables. I believe the great question of the twenty-first century is the question of how we "be" together. Not how we *are* together or how we *relate to* one another, but how our state of being, our very essence, touches one another and learns to thrive in a state of interdependence. Those suppers served as an important counterpoint to the broader public narrative of division that continues to unfold. I write to you now just months after another presidential election threatens to break our country in ways not seen since the Civil War. Followers of the outgoing president, drunk off conspiratorial lies that the election was somehow stolen, violently stormed the United States Capitol, resulting in the death of five of their fellow citizens. The episode lays bare just how fundamentally vulnerable our democracy is.

Everything feels deeply precarious. Calls for unity and appeals to our better angels seem to ring hollow when there is a threat that our nation will become a failed state. Yet, I still long for a community that will not be found in shallow platitudes promoting reconciliation. It will require the courage of everyday heroes to dig deep and find within themselves the wherewithal to lean into one another and repair the breach of relationships currently exposed.

I believe this will look different from community to community. For some who have experienced the worst of the bigotry, hatred, and violence of this moment, it feels unethical to ask them to bridge with those who do not affirm their humanity. For them, this is a moment of turning inward and finding fortification within their communities. Many of us whose identities place us at the margins rightly fear for our lives. In the absence of safe spaces, we need to create brave spaces of collective healing and fortification that will thicken our relationships with each other and ensure that we can withstand the difficult days ahead.

For others, the call is to create bridges across lines of difference. This bridge-building work is at its core an act of radical hope *and* hospitality. As Priscilla Shirer reminds us, it is not an invitation into a vision of unity through sameness. Instead, it invites us to lean into our radical differences by inviting strangers to lean into vulnerability and share the truth of their life experiences—their hurts, challenges, joys, and concerns—to uncover the humanity in each of us. It also will require loving accountability to call out patterns of behavior that can be harmful and destructive to the livelihoods of others.

There is a temptation in these bridging spaces, particularly among my white liberal friends, to only want to bridge with those whose difference is discernible to the human eye. To them I say, for the sake of your beloved human siblings, particularly those of color who do not yet have the emotional space to be your teachers—please take this moment as an opportunity to also bridge with those whose diversity is not as visibly acute.

For those in urban areas, that means bridging with rural communities. For those who carry educational privilege, it means listening to those without a college degree and recognizing the knowledge gleaned from their experiences as valid and true. For those with family members of a different political party, bridge building means practicing deep listening skills that give space to take their viewpoints and concerns into account.

I have a friend who is fond of saying it's hard to build a bridge in the middle of a flood. So, when people ask me how to begin this constructive work of building bridges, I invite them to answer these three questions:

- **What are you bridging toward?** Being clear about your commitments and intentions is fundamental in developing trust. When we are clear about what we are seeking to accomplish together we can manage our expectations accordingly.

- **What are you bridging over?** The history of the United States is messy, complicated, and violent. Bridging work requires that we do not avert our eyes from the truth of stories, but rather that we honor that which is before us.

- **What is your bridge made of?** I don't know about you, but if I am going to work across differences to confront the horrors of white supremacy and a legacy of systemic inequality, I want a bridge built of steel, not sticks. It requires that each of us does our work to understand where our pain points are and how we need to sharpen our skills to listen with empathy and grace to the person sitting across from us.

The movement between building bridges and brave spaces is not static but fluid. Some of us will move between both worlds. Some will invest in only one. None of us can do it all, which is why we need each other. Let us call one another into a space of moral courage and hold each other well. What ails our nation will not be solved by electoral politics; it can only be solved by strengthening our relationships to one another. The ancestors are watching and waiting for our response.

Love,

A Woman Who Loves to Eat

Hold Each Other Tight and Pull Back the Veil

A Letter to My Little Cousins[31]

Dear Beloved,

Hear these words from *New York Times* best-selling writer adrienne maree brown, "Things are not getting worse, they are getting uncovered. we must hold each other tight and continue to pull back the veil."[32]

I don't know about you, but the suggestion that things are not getting worse comes as a surprise. Each day we are inundated with images, videos, and words from screens and social media feeds about how divided we are and questions about whether our nation will be able to survive the cultural stress test that we are placing on our institutions. The message is clear: These are dark days, the likes of which we have never seen in our nation's 240-plus years.

Yet, we have inhabited darkness before. On the fields of Gettysburg and at the F.W. Woolworth lunch counter in Greensboro. We

---

[31] This letter was adopted from a speech written and delivered by Jennifer Bailey at the Elon University Baccalaureate ceremony on May 23, 2019. As of June 28, 2021, the full address can be found online at https://www.elon.edu/u/news/2019/05/23/the-rev-jennifer-bailey-encourages-graduates-to-show-up-and-lead/

[32] adrienne maree brown, "Living through the Unveiling," February 3, 2017, http://adriennemareebrown.net/2017/02/03/living-through-the-unveiling.

have forced native sons and daughters to walk a Trails of Tears in the name of manifest destiny, exploited laborers in the name of economic progress, and placed our citizens in internment camps in the name of national security. When I listen closely, I can hear the voices of our ancestors crying out from the soil across time with one voice, "Remember! Remember!"

This call to remembrance may feel counterintuitive to us in the United States because embedded within our country's DNA is a cultural incentive to forget. So much of our nation's self-understanding is rooted in a misguided conception of American Exceptionalism. This notion holds that we, as a nation, are uniquely virtuous among all nations—that our values, system of governance, and history have set us apart, thus making us worthy of universal admiration and praise. From a young age, this ideal is poured into us through our textbooks and classroom assignments. Our educational system is as much about training us to be "good citizens" as it is about teaching us how to read and write.

To be clear, there is absolutely nothing wrong with being proud of where we come from. Our identities are inevitably tied to the people and places that we call home. Nor is there an inherent problem in wanting our children to be equipped through their schooling to be good and decent members of society—or put simply, not jerks.

A problem emerges when we begin to conflate a commitment to this exceptionalist ideal with our sense of patriotism. This can lead down a perilous path and blind us to those parts of our collective narrative that are unflattering or downright horrific. It can distort our minds into believing that dissent is problematic when we know that some of the best moments of the American story emerged when patriots saw a societal ill causing harm to others and sought to change it.

There is power in memory. That is why I believe that the ancestors continue to call us to it.

Indeed, it is the only antidote to the silence and forgetfulness of death. I believe that this call to memory is not just about naming the pain of the past, but also about capturing the stories of joy, resilience, and hope that also are part of our history.

We are living in apocalyptic times. The apocalypse I have in mind is not the summer blockbuster image of the end of days brought about by an alien, viral, or nuclear attack. Rather, we are in a period of remaking the world as we know it. Indeed, the Greek root of the word "apocalypse" means to uncover.

Regardless of where you fall on the ideological spectrum or how you cast your vote, one thing is exceedingly clear: The past several years have uncovered and exposed a rupture at the very heart of our democracy. It is a rupture rooted in the deep paralysis of anxiety and disparate visions for our collective future. The very systems that once provided meaning are dying around us. Good factory jobs with union wages are gone. Membership in many religious communities is dwindling. Like any festering wound, the past several years have exposed just how fragile and frayed the ties that bind our republic really are.

Gen Z, you had a front row seat to the uncoverings of this era. The conditions of your lives were shaped against the backdrop of these great existential crises. One of the things I admire most about you is the pragmatic idealism with which you approach the challenges before us. Like generations of young people who came before you, you are not afraid to question authority or the status quo. At the same time, you understand that the issues, from climate change to public health, have the potential to shape the world irreversibly.

As hopeless as these times may seem, the Christian tradition teaches me that out of death there is the possibility of new life.

Cynicism is the easy option. To be snarky and fatalistic about the conditions before us is not cool. It's lazy. Radical hope—the type that actually requires us to take an active role in shaping the better future we want to see—is far more difficult. It requires us to put some skin in the game.

So as you prepare to step into adulthood, and you stare into the chasm of endless possibility that is the future, you can rest in the fact that you are not alone as you embark into the great unknown. There are people at your front, back, and sides who will walk with you as you ask questions, make mistakes, and go about continuing the work that is living your life.

I personally can vouch for this fact. Ten years ago, I was in your shoes. I was preparing as you are today to launch into what my advisors, parents, and professors kept calling "the real world." That concept, I would soon find out, was a lie. Certainly, the bubble of my campus life shielded me from the devastating reality check that was my bank account balance after my first round of rent and utility bills. But I am here to affirm that you have indeed been living in the real world. The heartbreaks, triumphs, struggles, and experiences of resilience that have occurred during your life thus far were not only real, but preparation for what is to come.

I write to you not as a wise elder sage speaking from on high, but as a big cousin, sister, or auntie. I am just a little bit farther down the road than you, still learning, growing, and anticipating who it is I will be when I grow up. Perhaps, I am like that cousin who is still with-it enough to know most artists on the top of the streaming charts, the one you go to for insight when parents just don't understand. You have my permission to take what is useful and leave the rest behind on your chairs.

I have been reflecting about the things I wish I had known when I was sitting in your seat, things like what it means to lead into the great unknown during radically uncertain times.

I believe that the American project is intentionally an unfinished one. Each generation is able to contribute to that vision by introducing that which is generative and new, while casting off that which has grown harmful and destructive. New voices emerge to help guide us in identifying and naming the great moral and human crises of our times.

I am a millennial. You, my beloved Gen Z, are not. Millennials are cartographers making maps. Millennials took stock of the shifting political, social, cultural, and economic landscapes that define our era through new technologies. Millennials created a blueprint for what our ideal communal life might be.

You are the builders.

You are the ones who will take the blueprint, revise it as necessary, and create the new structures that will sustain us into the future.

What I've learned along the way is that *what* you build is less important than *how* you build it. In particular, it is the act of investing time, commitment, and energy into your relationships with family, friends, and colleagues that will make all the difference.

I have found in my work that relationships move at the speed of trust and social change moves at the speed of relationships.

Sometimes the urgency of the moment requires us to respond and move swiftly to attend to the real life-and-death challenges that confront us. The changes to our climate and growing threat of white nationalist violence are pressing issues that are shaping our future in real time.

Yet more often than not, most of our lives are spent in the in-between times—those moments of mundanity between major milestones. Please know there will be those in your life who will attempt to pressure you to move professionally and personally at a pace that advances *their* goals but leave you feeling depleted, exhausted, and burnt out. I am here today to tell you that while fanning the flames of your ambition, it's okay to pause and take a breath. It's okay to spend time sowing seeds of relationship and nurture in yourself and your community.

Our communities are the people we practice doing life with. They are the imperfect folks who call us back to ourselves when we have lost our way, the people to whom we are most accountable, and who love us through our messiness and mistakes. Cultivating a community takes time and investment. But when the inevitability of loss and grief, heartache and pain occur, those relationships have the power to sustain us and see us through. When you get that big promotion, find the love of your life, or just discover a favorite new song on Spotify, they are the people who will dance with you, celebrate you, and toast your success.

The shape of that community will change over time as old friends exit and new ones enter.

There will be faces in this crowd that you will never see again after tomorrow and others that you will find again in unexpected places and moments along life's journey.

You will change over time.

The currents of your experiences will be like waves against stone, shaping the precious gift that is your one life into something that is uniquely yours alone.

The world will change.

New technologies, geo-political conflicts, pop culture moments, and natural disasters will shape the world in ways that we cannot yet imagine.

As the science fiction writer Octavia Butler reminds us:

All that you touch you change.

All that you change, changes you.

The only lasting truth is change.

God is change.[33]

Yet if we continue to hold each other tight and pull back the veil, perhaps we can be active participants in guiding and shifting that change to move in a direction that opens the door to more love, peace, equity, and justice for each living thing and the planet that sustains us.

Despite the uncertainty, rhetoric of division, and noise that is so dominant in the public narrative of this moment, we have the power to shape the story that we want to tell our children and great-grandchildren about how we showed up and led into this period of the great unknown.

To again quote adrienne maree brown, "things are not getting worse, they are being uncovered. hold each other tight and pull back the veil."

Love,

An Auntie in Training

---

[33] Octavia E. Butler, *Parable of the Sower* (New York: Grand Central Publishing 2nd Edition, 2019), 3.

Post-Script

Beloved,

I hope that my letters have been an entry point to your own story and an invitation to reflect on the themes of faith, race, loss and radical hope that have been so important in my own journey. As you consider these topics, I invite you to pick up a pencil or pen and write to someone who is beloved to you. It can be someone you have never met, a cherished friend, a historical figure, or a dear one who has yet to be born who embodies these themes to you.

Below are a few prompts, inspired by our work with the People's Supper to help get you started.

Faith

From the People's Supper *Faith-Based Supper Add-On*

- Who is someone you know, a historical figure, or a figure from your faith tradition/scriptures who models radical hope?

- What is a spiritual practice or ritual that gives you strength when times are hard?

- What stories from your tradition inspire you to be your most courageous self?

- Who and what do you hold sacred?

Race[34]

For People of Color

- Describe your first experience of racial injustice or discrimination. How did it shape your worldview?

- As we think about the moment that we're in, the pain that led us here, and this history and manifestation of racial injustice in our community, where does it hurt?

- What do you love most about being a part of your community?

- Tell a story from your upbringing that gives us a picture of your first experience with community. What was positive in this? And what can you now see that it was missing? How does this set you up for your own hopes for building community? A neighborhood? A country?

For White Folks

- Describe a time when you first realized you were white. What did this experience teach you?

- How did your parents and family raise you to see race, your whiteness, and the history of racism within the United States?

- What is an issue related to race that you don't understand and would like to understand but feel uncomfortable bringing up/not knowing about?

- Imagine you're talking to your grandchildren or great-grandchildren. What story do you want to be able to

---

[34] From the People's Supper Guidebook *A Racial Justice Journey: Looking in, Looking Out, and Mapping a Path to Change.* https://static1.squarespace.com/static/595e51dbd1758e528030285b/t/5f721b9838eddc5c29cf7e83/1601313708177/RacialJusticeGuidebook_FinalSept2020.pdf.

tell them about what you did in this moment in the story of racial justice?

Loss

- Describe an experience of loss that left you changed. How are you different now than you were before?

- Reflect on a person you loved and lost. Write three tiny letters to yourself, sharing lessons and words you've held onto, or words you wish they'd shared, or words you'd like to pass forward.[35]

- Share the things that matter most with the people who matter most to you. After working with hundreds of dying patients, renowned palliative care doctor Ira Byock found that there were just four things that patients and their families alike needed to say and to hear: "I love you," "thank you," "I'm sorry," and "please forgive me." Use the prompts above to write a letter to someone living, or to the dead, or from the perspective of the dead, giving yourself the words you need to hear.

- Share a story of joy about time spent with someone who you miss.

Radical Hope

- What makes you feel deeply alive?

- What is the vision of hope that sustains you?

- Who or what makes you feel most rooted?

- How do you practice hope in your life each day?

---

[35] The Dinner Party, *Happy F***king Holidays: A Guide for Gathering*, https://static1.squarespace.com/static/5b1066184611a029fec8f7c4/t/5fbeaaf-52dd96f5918cc7956/1606331132647/happyfuckingholidays+11.2020.pdf, 12.

Acknowledgements

This work was a labor of love that would not have been possible without the consistent support and steadfast encouragement of my community.

I am overwhelmed with **gratitude for**

...the church women, past and present, of the Bethel AME Church (Quincy, Illinois), Greater Institutional AME Church (Chicago, Illinois), and Greater Bethel AME Church (Nashville, Tennessee) who taught me the meaning of radical hope.

...my mentors, living and dead, who nurtured me in my call and continue to encourage me at every step of my journey especially Alisa del Tufo, Rev. Dr. Dale Andrews, Eboo Patel, the Rev. Dr. Emilie Townes, Rev. Diane Bogues, Rev. Dr. John Vaughn, Katrina Moore, Krista Tippett, Lisa Anderson, Rev. Mac Pendleton, Rev. Matthew Wesley Williams, Rev. Michael Broadnax, Rev. Pattie Hardimon, Rev. Dr. Reginald Blout, Shifra Bronznick, Taina Mc-Field, Rev. Dr. Walter B. Johnson Jr., and Rev. Walter W. Reid Jr.

...my Faith Matters Network family, past and present, who inspire me to plant seeds of radical hope each day. Anna Del Castillo, Brittney Jackson Brown, Carinne Luck, Gloria Winston-Harris, Hilary Allen, Jemma Suwa, Margaret Ernst, Micky ScottBey Jones, Rachel Kipnes, Rachel Terns, and Ristina Gooden thank you for growing something beautiful with me.

... the faith leaders, organizers, movement chaplains, healers, and activists that are the heart and soul of our work at Faith Matters Network walking alongside and learning with you is the honor of my life.

...sisters and brothers in ministry and seminary comrades who expanded my vision of who God can be. Aaliyah Hunt, Aaron Stauffer, Angie Thurston, Boyce Wilkins, Candace Perkins, Casper ter Kuile, Cecily Randle, Chelsea Yarborough, Courtney Bryant, Eric Brown, Gregory Barker, K Scarry, Kevin Brown, Kyle Brooks, Leonard Curry, Lora Andrews, Lucas Johnson, Michael Fisher, Michelle Wyatt, Nicholas Hayes, Rachel Kinney, Sarah Pinson, Terrell Hunt, and Prisca Dorcas Mojica Rodriguez thank you for letting the Divine shine through you so brightly.

...the sister-friends who have danced, wept, and laughed with me into womanhood. Bre Detwiler, C.J. Thayer, Danielle Allen, Dionne Maynor, Dom Johnson, Geoanna Bautista, Helen Hare, Jennifer McClendon, Jordan Heard, Juliana Lindsey, Lennon Flowers, Marcia Lee, Megan Black, Megan Lubin, Nhu-Y Ngo, Olusola Tribble, Sonia Sarkar, Teneice Wesson, and Tya Winn I love you.

...my chosen family who became ancestors too soon, Glendon-Tyler Ashmon and Josephine Chow, who continue to teach me from the other side.

....my family of origin - my aunties, uncles, and cousins- for loving me then, loving me now, and loving me always.

....my grandmothers and great-grandmothers Harriet, Helen, Martha Ann, Roberta, and Vera for the resilience and strength that I inherited from each of you.

....Dori Baker, who would not let me give up on the possibility of this book.

....my daddy, Keith, who passed down to me a love for the written word, learning, and laughter.

....**my mama, Christine**, who continues to be my guiding light and compass.

...**my baby Max** for bringing fresh joy into my life every day.

...**my husband, Ira Helderman**, who is himself a healer who is teaching me more about the depth and width of love than anyone. Thank you for joining me on this life journey, I could not do it without you.

About the Series

Cultivating Faithful, Wise, and Courageous Leaders for the Church and Academy

Welcome to a conversation at the intersection of young adults, faith, and leadership. The Forum for Theological Exploration (FTE) is a leadership incubator that inspires diverse young people to make a difference in the world through Christian communities. This series, published in partnership with Chalice Press, reimagines Christian leadership and creates innovative approaches to ministry and scholarship from diverse contexts.

These books are written by and for a growing network of:

- Partners seeking to cultivate the Christian leaders, pastors, and theological educators needed to renew and respond to a changing church.
- Young leaders exploring alternative paths to ministry and following traditional ways of serving the common good—both inside and beyond "the walls" of the church and theological academy.
- Christian leaders developing new ways to awaken the search for meaning and purpose in young adults who are inspired to shape the future.
- Members of faith communities creating innovative solutions to address the needs of their congregations, institutions, and the broader community.

This series offers an opportunity to discover what FTE is learning, widen the circle of conversation, and share ideas FTE believes are necessary for faith communities to shape a more hopeful future. Authors' expressed ideas and opinions in this series are their own and do not necessarily reflect the views of FTE.

Thank you for joining us!

Dori Baker, Series Editor
Stephen Lewis, FTE President

Other books from the
Forum for Theological Exploration

Faith and Ferguson:
Sparking Leadership and Awakening Community
by Leah Gunning Francis

Nobody Cares When We Die:
God, Community, and Surviving to Adulthood
by Patrick Reyes

Stakes Is High:
Race, Faith, and Hope for America
by Michael W. Waters

Another Way:
Living and Leading Change on Purpose
by Stephen Lewis, Matthew Wesley Williams,
and Dori Grinenko Baker

Staying Awake:
The Gospel for Changemakers
by Tyler Sit

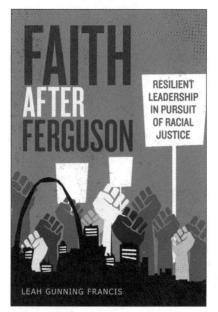

9780827211445, $18.99

"*Faith after Ferguson* focuses on the importance of putting religious teachings into action for the greater good. Though its subject matter is difficult, *Faith after Ferguson*, with its numerous examples of faith leaders and communities stepping up to fight for racial justice, should also be a source of comfort and inspiration on the long road ahead."

—*Foreword Reviews*

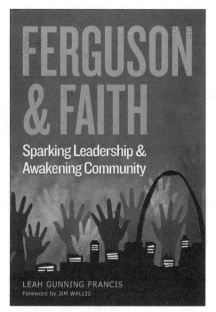

9780827211056, $19.99

The Ferguson protests represented a long-smoldering movement for justice. Seminary professor, Leah Gunning Francis was among the activists, and her interviews with more than two dozen faith leaders and with the new movement's organizers take us behind the scenes of the continuing protests.

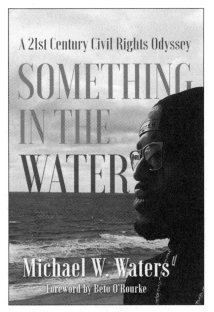

9780827235496, $16.99

"Waters, an African American pastor and civil rights activist, delivers a blistering critique of white supremacy and racial injustice in this trenchant collection of sermons, poems, and commentaries. This concise, incisive work should be a wake-up call to Americans in general and the church in particular."

—*Publishers Weekly*

9780827200999, $17.99

"*Anxious To Talk About It* is challenging, encouraging, and always faithful. Helsel's insight and wisdom strengthens our discipleship and helps us confront the impact of racism through gratitude, gift appreciation, diversity, and self-control. This book is a must-read for anyone desiring to live a spiritual life of self-discovery in the 21st century."

—Jimmie Hawkins, Director of the Presbyterian Church (USA) Office of Public Witness & United Nations

chalice press
You Want to Change the World. So Do We.

Order at ChalicePress.com or wherever you buy books.

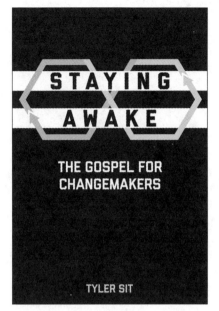

9780827235526, $16.99

"An eloquent debut...Sit's work sizzles with energy, humor, and empathy. This impressive guide conveys urgent, timely guidance for pastors, Christians, and seekers looking to marry faith and social justice."

—*Publishers Weekly*
  (STARRED REVIEW)

chalice press
You Want to Change the World. So Do We.

**Order at ChalicePress.com
or wherever you buy books.**